THE SKY IS FALLING!?!

A PROPOSAL FOR LEADERSHIP COMMUNITIES
TO TAKE NEW RISKS FOR THE REIGN OF GOD.

THE SKY IS FALLING!?!

LEADERS LOST IN TRANSITION

ALAN J. ROXBURGH

Foreword by: BRIAN D. McLAREN

ACI Publishing

EAGLE, IDAHO

Published in Eagle, Idaho, by ACI Publishing

PO Box 639
Eagle, ID 83616

Manuscript prepared by Rick Killian, Killian Creative, Boulder, Colorado.
www.killiancreative.com

Design + Production: Lookout Design, Inc., Stillwater, Minnesota

ISBN 0-9777184-0-9

Printed in the United States of America

06 07 08 09 10 11 12 13   10 9 8 7 6 5 4 3 2 1

Category Christian Living/Business & Leadership

CONTENTS

FOREWORD

I've just finished reading (and enjoying) the book you are now about to read and enjoy. Like you, I am encountering this book at a certain point in my life, and my current experience affects the way I am processing its contents. In particular, two things are happening in my life these days that this book has addressed in a very deep way.

First, in recent months, as a person associated with the group Alan here identifies as "Emergents," I have been experiencing some criticism from people whose approach to faith might be called (unhelpfully, as Alan will point out) "institutional." To be frank, I've felt a mixture of discouragement, anger, anxiety, and confusion in discerning how to respond to these criticisms. Reading the chapters you're about to begin, I found myself somehow calmed. I was reminded again that we—meaning all of us engaged in the Christian community in its many forms—are passing through change and experiencing transition, and that a certain amount of critique, defense, counter-critique, blame, and frustration is inevitable. I felt Alan was helping me get my bearings in the midst of stressful times and experiences.

Second, in the coming months, I will be passing the baton of leadership in the church I helped plant twenty-three years ago. I hope to stay involved in this community of faith in which my children have been raised, and in which my wife and I have done what has been up to now our main life's work. I hope it will be, for some years at least, our home base and our faith community, but soon I will no longer be the senior pastor. I am not sad about this change. It comes "in the fullness of time" for me, and I am especially excited because I'm thrilled about the new young leader who will soon be my pastor and whose leadership I will be privileged to support as I serve on his team. Many times as I read this book, I felt profoundly grateful that my successor will have the book you are now holding to help him—and our whole leadership team—to continue to engage wisely with these challenging, liminal (or threshold) times. And of course, I also felt grateful that I will be able to recommend it to the leaders I will continue to serve in my own ministry in the years ahead.

Your responses to this book will no doubt be affected by where you are—whether you identify more as "Liminal" or "Emergent," whether you are working in an existing church or a newly forming one. But I am confident that you will feel, as I do, that this book is one of the most important you have read in a long time—especially if you read it with the thoughtfulness it deserves.

Alan has been a friend and mentor to me for some years now. Only a few years my senior, I feel he is many years wiser. Anyone who meets Al soon realizes he is brilliant. Even if he is silent, his flashing eyes tell you he has an active mind, and his brain is nearly always storming with creativity and insight. But in this book, I realized as never before how compassionate he is. He feels the pain of Liminals grappling with loss and anxiety and dislocation over the changes that surge around us like tidal waves, disembedding us from firm footing and taking us in dizzying chaos to who-knows-where. And he also feels the pain of Emergents—more ready to leave the past behind, perhaps, but in leaving it, we find ourselves in danger of losing much of what we need to face an unknown future. He understands how both groups need mentors to help us understand the chaos so we won't blame one another or in other ways part company; he sees how, in fact, we Liminals and Emergents actually need one another as never before. I believe he is right on all counts.

I began writing my first book just ten years ago. Because there were so few books like the one you're now holding back then, I was writing largely from hunches and instinct (and, one hopes, some kind of gracious guidance and discernment). Ten years of experience suggests I got at least one thing right: the first chapter of that book was entitled *Maximize Discontinuity*. In this book, Alan helps us understand why today's cultural and strategic discontinuities cannot be minimized, why small or cosmetic changes won't suffice, and why strategic planning won't get us from Stage One to Stage Five of change (something you'll soon learn about).

You'll also learn about continuous and discontinuous change, about frames and frameworks, about the new/ancient kinds of leaders needed in times like these, about the possibilities of missional orders led by abbots and abbesses who know how to function as "Synergists." You'll see what is to me a fresh and hopeful way of engaging with the Scriptures—not in a dismissive "they're irrelevant" way nor in a fundamentalist "chapter-and-verse" way, but in a profound, reverent, narrative way that discovers exactly the generative resources needed in times like ours.

All of this will be presented in understandable and sometimes very visual ways, employing metaphors ranging from family, work, forestry, engineering, business, cultural anthropology, to much more. Through it all, two things, I hope, will become more and more clear to more and more of us. First, if we need new kinds of churches, we cannot develop them with old kinds of leaders. We ourselves need to become those new kinds of leaders, even as we all look to the next generations to help them be formed in new apprenticeships in the kinds of skills that Alan here describes.

But if that's all we realize, we're missing what may be Alan's most radical and powerful insight of all: *having new kinds of churches with new kinds of leaders is not the point.* In the end, even though we in the church talk and talk (and write and write) about church, church, church, church . . . it's not about the church. The church exists for something bigger than itself. Understanding that one thing alone will be worth your expense, time, and effort in turning this page and reading on—with an open mind and an open heart.

Brian McLaren
Laurel, Maryland
August 2005

PREFACE

MISSIONAL—
WHAT'S IN A WORD?

For ten years now as a pastor and a teacher, I have been involved in a discussion about changes in the Western church that has slowly become known as the "missional" conversation. As culture transforms, so must our language to engage it. The word *missional* evolved in just this way.

The idea was first fully articulated when the book *Missional Church: A Vision for the Sending of the Church in North America* was published in 1998. Its beginnings lay in the writing of Bishop Lesslie Newbigin, who had been a missionary in India for over thirty years. Newbigin, upon his retirement in the late 1960s, returned to his native England to encounter the fact that the Christian soul of the Western culture he'd left thirty years earlier had all but disappeared. Newbigin saw that, by the late twentieth century, the greatest challenge to the Gospel was no longer the unreached masses of the world, but the peoples of Europe and North America who had rapidly lost their Christian identity. In a memorable epithet, Newbigin asked: *Can the West be converted?* That question expressed one of the fundamental issues of the missional quest: *the challenge facing the European and North American churches was the re-conversion of its own people.*

This new view of the church as needing to be *missional* struck a note in the churches of North America as well and quickly became the *lingua franca* of many church leaders. The missional conversation might have died and disappeared like so many other concepts and movements of the church had there not been such a strong underlying sense at the time that something was indeed amiss about Christian life and identity in our society. The values that were central to our churches in years past—namely, "what God was calling us to do for others"—had drastically changed to, "what am I going to get out of coming to church?" The message of Christ being preached from our pulpits was changing accordingly and has become radically different from what was preached even half a century ago. We are in a period of massive change and upheaval. In this context, the missional conversation has given us useful language to discuss and address the challenges facing what it means to be a "Christian" in our time.

The word *missional* was coined to express the conviction that North America and Europe are now primary "mission fields" themselves. *Missional* also expresses that *God's mission* (or *missio dei* as we will later explore it) is that which shapes and defines all that the church is and does, as opposed to expecting church to be the ultimate self-help group for meeting our own needs and finding fulfillment in our individual lives. If the West is once again a mission field within which the central narratives of the gospel have been either lost or profoundly compromised by other values, then the focus of this *mission* must be upon placing the God who has encountered us in Jesus Christ back in the center of our communities of faith that shape and give meaning to our lives. This may seem an obvious part of being a Christian, but it is not happening in our American churches today.

Throughout Western societies, and most especially in North America, there has occurred a fundamental shift in the understanding and practice of the Christian story. It is no longer about God and what God is about in the world; it is about how God serves and meets human needs and desires. It is about how the individual self can find its own purposes and fulfillment. More specifically, our churches have become spiritual food courts for the personal, private, inner needs of expressive individuals. The result is a debased, compromised, derivative form of Christianity that is not the gospel of the Bible at all. The biblical narrative is about God's mission in, through, and for the sake of the world and how God has called human beings to be part of God's reaching out to that world for God's purpose of saving it in love. The focus of attention should be what God wants to accomplish and how we can be part of

God's mission, not how God helps us accomplish our own agendas.

This is why the way we conduct church is such an essential part of the missional conversation. God intended the local church to be a *sign, witness,* and *foretaste* of where God is inviting all creation to Himself through Jesus Christ. The ways of the church are to be a contrast to the ways of the world—it is intended to be strikingly different from the immediate society around it. The church is to be formed around beliefs and practices discovered through interaction with scripture and not primarily derived from the particular culture in which it is found, although it must also be embodied in translatable forms within a culture. We are to be in the world, but not of it—we are to give it meaning and purpose, not pull our meaning and purposes from it.

This book is about the challenges facing church leaders who want to embark on the missional quest to return the God we encounter in Christ back to the center of what being a Christian is all about. What I have learned over these ten years is that the missional agenda can never take root and flourish without attention to the practical issues of how we lead in such a time of great change. Already, the missional conversation has been engaged with those of two other movements that we will address in detail in the following chapters—the Postmodern and the Emergent. The fact that we have so many different conversations happening at once indicates the levels of flux and struggle that exist today as we seek to understand the nature of faithful Christian witness in our time. In the language and conversations of the postmodern and emerging church groups, we also find a clash with the traditional methods that have served Western churches for so long. This is a time when many in existing congregations and denominations are unsure of the way ahead, while a growing number of younger leaders are jettisoning the established forms of church life in the belief that these wineskins can no longer carry us forward into the new places God wants us to go. Is such radical change demanded, or are we throwing the proverbial baby out with the bathwater?

Personally, I am one who cannot easily lay aside the traditions and life of existing congregations, but at the same time my affinities are with many of the emergent leaders, their instincts, passions, and creativity. I don't share the critiques of many that traditional systems are so hopelessly compromised that they are totally obsolete and must be completely replaced with new methods. I know that much of what is traditional is there for a purpose, and we stand to lose greatly if we so easily reject what was learned along the journey to where we are today. I am disappointed by the false dichotomies between "organized" and "organic" church. This is nonsense. The conviction of this book is: that both the emergent and traditional churches need each other and have much to learn from one another; that in our willingness to struggle together, we will be given an imagination from the Spirit that is bigger than all our assumptions, positions, and strategies; and that if that spirit of working together is compromised, all of us will lose.

All of this leads to why I feel the need to continue the missional conversation with this book: while many good things are coming out of our willingness to address the unique needs of our Western culture at the dawn of the twenty-first century, we must also discern and hold fast to the best of what has gotten us here. It is not time for these movements to divide and go separate ways, but it is time for each to come together afresh and see where God is leading by inspiring new language to both understand and minister to our world. Thus I ask you to read the following pages not as a student of my thoughts, but as a fellow traveler seeking where God is leading us together. If our land and culture is again a mission field, it will take all of us to reach it. It is time to again seek and embrace God's mission for our lives so that we can truly transform our communities with the gospel of Jesus Christ.

Alan J. Roxburgh
August 2005

ACKNOWLEDGMENTS

This book is the result of many generous gifts of friendship over the past number of years. A person is formed out of the relationships that shape his life, and I am deeply grateful for many people who have shaped mine as well as contributed to the shaping of this work.

First I want to mention Pat Keifert and Mark Priddy. I met Mark a little less than two years ago and was immediately aware of a man in whom God's love and grace was not only present, but shared generously for the sake of the kingdom. I want to thank Mark for making it possible for me to take a summer to work on this book. I want to also thank him for his vision and commitment to developing structures and opportunities for the ongoing work of understanding and discerning the nature of missional leadership.

Pat Keifert is a unique man whose intellectual capacities and loyal friendship have been an important part of my own learning and development in the past few years. His friendship and partnership have been an important ingredient in my writing. Pat is one of those few, gifted people whose life and passion is focused toward amplifying the glory of God in the world. I am deeply grateful for his wisdom and friendship over these past years. It has been a great privilege for me to share this journey of understanding and forming missional life with Pat.

Above all, I want to acknowledge and thank my wife, Jane, for her deep love and amazing partnership with me over these many years. She has been the one who has anchored my life as I've traveled the world sharing these ideas and seeking to put them into practice. There aren't words to express how important and basic her love and support have been.

For those who may see their ideas in this book and fail to find an acknowledgement—let me apologize from the start. I am grateful to you all and know the book is better for the conversations we have had together, but don't have the room here to thank all of you adequately. May you still be richly blessed for all you have contributed to this work as well as my life.

SECTION ONE

LOST IN TRANSITION

TWO TRIBES IN A STRANGE NEW WORLD

There's something about the opening to the movie *Seabiscuit* that draws me in every time I see it. It's a simple scene, really. A man, wearing a shop apron and gaiters to protect his shirtsleeves, loiters outside a new business: C. S. Howard's Bicycles—a modest storefront where bicycles are sold and repaired. There's just one problem—Charles Howard has no customers. In fact, viewers soon see Charles dozing on a bench, waiting for business that never materializes. People wander by, and carriages fill the streets, but no one, it seems, is interested in the expertise this aspiring entrepreneur has to offer.

Then, suddenly, Charles's fortunes change. A man pulls up driving a Stanley automobile with steam billowing from under its hood. "The boiler blew on me," says the driver. "Can you fix it?" Charles thinks for a moment and then responds with a confident, "Sure." In true movie fashion, an inspired Charles not only manages to fix the strange new machine, but dramatically improves its performance as well. As a result, he abandons the bicycle business to become a highly successful automotive dealer.

I don't know about you, but I can relate to that scene. No, I've never worked in a bicycle repair shop, but I do know what it's like to feel hopelessly out of touch. And, chances are, you do as well.

The truth is many Christian leaders today feel like the owners of such bicycle repair shops, waiting for business. Not long ago, it seemed everyone was riding bicycles and there was a significant demand for trained professionals in the field of bicycle maintenance. But today, the primary form of transportation has changed. New machines are rolling up to our front doors and deep down we know that we have no idea how to respond to this new reality. For many people, this is a confusing, frustrating place to be.

Changing Times Require New Strategies

As church leaders today, it's as if we've been trained to fix bicycles. In many cases, it's the only thing we know how to do. We're good at it and we have a suitcase full of special tools to help us accomplish this task. We have letters after our names that validate our skills, and titles that identify us as certified experts. The only problem is, no one cares anymore. Our frameworks seem disconnected from the emerging cultural context, and our words are often received as a strange, foreign language. We read books about becoming a new kind of Christian, or becoming more mission-directed, but we're not sure what exactly needs to change. A bomb, of sorts, has gone off in our hearts and we've become aware that something is amiss, but practically speaking, we don't know what to do about it. We sense that a missional direction is right, but we feel unequal to the challenge. The leap from bicycles to cars seems too great.

This is the experience of what I call *liminality*[1]—or what Merriam-Webster's defines as "the condition of being on a threshold or at the beginning of a process."

---

[1] See also: Alan Roxburgh, *The Missionary Congregation, Leadership, & Liminality* (Harrisburg, PA: Trinity Press International, 1997).

Meanwhile, other leaders among us are experiencing a different kind of change-induced stress. These are people who have never known anything but change in their lives. Weary of fighting internal battles about meaning, control, and power, they've all but given up on existing church structures, believing them to be *institutional*, archaic, and out of touch with the demands of today's postmodern culture.[2]

Many of these people are no longer willing to jump through denominational hoops in order to be recognized as leaders. They believe such hoops no longer make sense in today's world. For them, seminary (or "cemetery" as some mockingly refer to it) education is suspect. It seems so distant and abstract. It demands that students be uprooted and placed in an unreal, disassociated, ivory tower environment for several years—only to end up serving in settings where, once again, they have no previous relationships.

Like the Liminals mentioned earlier, these Emergent leaders are also confused and frustrated. Although they long to contribute to a new kind of church, they find themselves without the guidelines, frameworks, and practices upon which to shape their vision. Reacting against what they see, they almost ritually confess to each other: "We don't know what we're doing, but of one thing we are sure: we're not going to form churches modeled after out-dated denominations and lifeless congregations."

THE TROUBLE WITH TRIBALISM

These two tribes, however, live in the same new world and are trying to reach the same culture. They are like next-door neighbors with a high fence built between them independently trying to invite their other

---

[2] In one sense these labels of the *institutional church* versus the *emergent church* are terribly unhelpful. To some extent the hearts of the Liminals and Emergents for a new kind of church are not that radically different in terms of the disciplines and thought they are contributing to the missional conversation. Tension, however, lies in how they address institutional arrangements. The Emergents seek to institute *alternative* arrangements, contrasting themselves with a so-called *institutional church*, however, all they are truly doing is replacing one set of institutional arrangements with another. All such paradoxical language only survives on the ability of people to simply accept it without questioning its assumptions. Here, however, we must go deeper than this.

neighbors to different block parties being held on the same Saturday afternoon. In many ways, they want the same things, but refuse to put aside their differences to work together against similar challenges to achieve those parallel visions.

This book is an attempt to unpack the challenges facing these two tribes and facilitate renewed dialogue between them. In fact, it's my conviction that without dialogue and cooperation between these two tribes—the *Liminals* and the *Emergents*—we will never be able to discern the shape of the communities God truly wants to call forth. Instead, we will continue to spin our wheels in us-versus-them rhetoric and miss the opportunity to discover the adaptive skills and imaginations *they* have and *we* need to form the new kingdom communities God is calling us to cultivate.

The fact is each tribe is trying to address similar questions of missional faithfulness in the midst of sweeping change. What's more, each tribe has the capacity to be a gift to the other. The problem is neither group is really listening or talking to the other.

For me, the picture became startlingly clear during a recent conference. In one room, a group of eight hundred to nine hundred young leaders sat dressed in T-shirts and blue jeans, blogging away on their Macs and participating in journey groups. Meanwhile, next door, a group of fourteen hundred to fifteen hundred Liminals wearing Polo shirts, Dockers, and loafers feverishly jotted down notes from the latest, greatest speaker on how to make their churches more effective. It wasn't just a generational difference either—each group had leaders of various ages. And while they were all attending the same conference, there was still virtually no sense of connection between the tribes.

Like it or not, members of the Liminal tribe carry with them the memory of important skills and habits, passed down through the generations, about how to form and lead God's people.[3] Although it's true that some denominational systems have become irrelevant in recent years, there still remains within these organizations traditions and history that are still essential for the formation of an emerging church today.

Similarly, the Emergent tribe is characterized by wonderful imagination and hope. Looking forward to a new kind of church, these men and women are willing to take great risks. They are brave, passionate people who long to experience God's missional life. The danger, of course, is that in jettisoning the church life they have known, they may unwittingly let go of crucial pieces of memory that can help lead them forward. Far too many are just reinventing the wheel—working hard to create new frameworks by which to define themselves—and are simply reproducing the frameworks and mistakes they so vehemently condemn in institutional churches.

We need to recognize that each tribe has gifts the other needs. Each requires the other to understand the nature of the changes we are all experiencing. The Liminals can receive from the Emergents their gifts of imagination, critical evaluation and feedback, and holy restlessness. The Emergents can receive from the Liminals the gifts of history, tradition, habits, capacities, and foundational theologies handed down to them through years of schooling and discipleship.

Not only do they need each other's gifts, but neither tribe on its own has the frameworks, skills, or capacities necessary to lead in the present reality. They both lack mentors. For each tribe, the challenge of the moment is to understand the nature of the changes we are encountering in our culture and to draw on each other's wisdom in learning how to develop leaders capable of meeting those challenges.

Wherein lies the second purpose of this book. The following pages are intended to help guide leaders through the change process itself.

---

[3] See Jane Jacobs' *Dark Ages Ahead* (Toronto: Random House Canada, 2004). The first chapter argues that a primary reason cultures fall into a dark age is not because there is a lack of earnest people striving to shape a better future, but because the culture has developed a state of collective amnesia in which the older stories, traditions, customs, and skills disappear from the collective abilities of people—they become like trees without roots, and soon collapse accordingly. We are facing something like this in the church today.

Whether one is a Liminal, an Emergent, or something in between (it's impossible to draw a definitive line between the two), I believe it's imperative that we develop a deeper understanding of the nature of change and learn to embrace its stages as part of God's divine engagement in our world. Without the language to make sense of the changes in our culture, we'll inevitably feel overwhelmed by, and even despairing over, our circumstances.

A few leaders, the elites in each tribe, will always shine in any circumstance. They will rise to the occasion and develop their own ways forward. However, the majority in each tribe must find ways of discovering and developing the frameworks and skills for leading in this new world. Without this, Liminals will become discouraged and cynical—some will drop out of the church to do something else with their lives; others will return to the old habits of chasing after the latest scheme or program that promises healthy church growth. Others will simply give up and sit it out until retirement. On the other hand, the Emergents will die out because the tribe was unable to develop habits that can be handed down. Some will leave, hurt and discouraged. Others will return to experimentation with little regard to what others had already tried before them. Others will, again, turn to new vocations.

It's my conviction that we need markers and pointers to guide our journeys. However, the first step in mapping any journey is to first figure out where you are at the moment. Before we can cultivate alternative imaginations, we need insight into the forces of change that are currently shaping our experience—forces that, until now, have seemed huge and unnameable. This book endeavors to provide leaders with usable and practical frameworks for naming and understanding these changes.

TWO CONVERSATIONS

I became acutely aware of the divergent worlds in which Liminals and Emergents live through two conversations I had recently.

While sitting in a restaurant in Adelaide, Australia with two thirty-something leaders after a conference, I was curious about how they were responding to what was happening in their lives and churches. Finally, in one question, one of them brought the entire discussion to its point: *How do you stay attentive to the Spirit when you are immersed in radical, discontinuous change all your life?*

As we talked, it became clear that the real challenge facing his generation was determining which changes to pay attention to. When sporadic, irregular change is accepted as the norm, the temptation is to deal with all change in the same way. The tendency is to take none of it seriously, he explained, and to see everything as novelty. This is a problem of discernment and judgment—how does one evaluate or even stop long enough to determine which changes to take seriously?

The other conversation I had was with a leader of a megachurch who was in his late forties. We met over lunch with several other church leaders to talk about a new initiative to bring several churches together. He wanted me to quickly and clearly spell out for him the benefits of involvement with the other denominational leaders around the table and what it would do for his church down the road. He described the growth of his church, the huge welcoming foyer with a new coffee shop, and all the preparation for the coming weekend's seeker-driven service of drama, contemporary music, and laid-back, non-confrontational teaching about how to make life work. Yet even in this well-strategized organization, something was missing.

Another man turned to me near the end of our meeting and also asked what he would be getting out of joining this new initiative. I explained as briefly as I could: *If you don't ask fundamental questions about what you're doing today, five years from now you will be doing exactly the same thing. You will have a huge front door attracting people on the basis of needs and a huge back door as they leave to go somewhere else to join the next new way of having their needs met. We have to address the question of how to form men and women who will live a committed Christian life now, next week, next month, and for the rest of their lives.*

Several days later I sat in a coffee bar with the senior pastor of that same church as he described the turmoil in his soul. He said, "We have poured our lives out to get this going over the last several years—we knew what we wanted and where we were going. Then, a few months ago I was standing in the pulpit on a Sunday morning preaching when it hit me in the guts. I knew, in an instant, that this is not what it's all about. I sensed deep inside that what we were about is not the direction of the kingdom. And I don't know what to do about it!"

Two different conversations—one with Emergents, the other with Liminals—both addressing the challenges of constant but irregular change in very different ways. The heart of the issue is: how can we be the church of Jesus in the midst of such continual, world-altering change?

REFLECTION AND APPLICATION

1. Where do you picture yourself along the Liminal-Emergent spectrum? What about your church? What skills, abilities, and offerings do you see in yourself and your church? Are there individuals at various places along the Liminal-Emergent spectrum in your own body of believers? How could you pull them together in your own church to discuss how your church is, might, and should address the North American change from a Christian culture to a new type of mission field?

2. What churches or groups in your community would be at the other end of the Liminal-Emergent spectrum? Are there already existing forums for you to broach discussing these issues with them, or will new ones need to be created? Make a list of action steps and ideas of how you might enter into such a discussion with different churches in your area.

3. Which do you feel your church needs the most: grounding and founding in doctrine, practice, or organization; or new methods of reaching out to your community in ways sensitive to our changing culture? Where can you go in your church or community to learn from others who are doing these things well? People are generally more apt to be interested in what you have to offer if you first show interest in learning from them—how could you use this principle to create dialogue and build relationships with other very different congregations in your community?

4. How do you see the cultural changes that have brought about the missional conversation specifically affecting your community? Is the soul of your community still Christian for the most part, or has it become something else? What do you think has allowed or brought these changes about? What relevance does the gospel of Jesus Christ have to your community?

5. In the introduction, we discussed that the missional conversation has emerged from the fact that today's postmodern churches are more focused on teaching people how God will help them find purpose and fulfillment in life than on teaching what God's plans and missions are for us and how we can be part of realizing them—do you agree or disagree with this? How is your church keeping Christ at the center of what it teaches Christianity is all about? How can you improve this focus?

BUT WHAT IF THE SKY *IS* FALLING?

Children everywhere are familiar with the story of Chicken Little. When an acorn drops on the head of the famous pullet, she is overwhelmed with emotion. "The sky is falling! The sky is falling!" she exclaims. "I must go tell the king."

And so Chicken Little runs toward the king's palace, telling everyone she meets along the way about her distressing discovery. Soon a gaggle of animal friends is running alongside her, equally unnerved. In fact, the group becomes so emotionally unglued that when a fox appears promising to show them a shortcut, they foolishly opt to follow him—not realizing he's leading them into his den—and an almost certain death.

This story highlights one of the difficulties we often have in responding to change, that is, seeing clearly what is actually happening. Are we dealing with a stray acorn or two, or the beginning of world-altering events? Our perception and understanding of the changes we face will ultimately determine our response.

The story of Chicken Little reminds me of the story of a pastor who began leading a congregation founded almost a hundred years earlier. When he arrived, one of the elders took him aside to give him a little

friendly advice. "With just a little more visitation and a few more programs, the church could revert back to the way it was twenty years ago,"
he suggested. This was a plea for comfortable, manageable, predictable
change—or what we might call *continuous change.* Like a single acorn, he
popped the pastor on the head and suggested change was needed, and
that with a few minor adjustments, it could be managed and the church
restored to its former glory.

Continuous change is comfortable change because it fits into our
prior understanding of the world. In this case, the elder sensed that
something had happened to his congregation, but he was certain a few
tweaks here and there could restore the church to its former luster.
Having been formed in a world that provided him with a guaranteed job
for life and routines that largely stayed the same year in and year out, his
confidence was rooted in his previous experience. Change was simple,
came about slowly, and you could manage and control it towards a
preferable end.

By contrast, if continuous change is comparable to a single acorn
hitting us on the head, *discontinuous change* is an all-out acorn assault.
Because there's no discernible pattern to the changes, the attacks seem
to come from all angles and directions. Discontinuous change literally
feels like the sky *is* falling. It exhausts our physical, mental, and spiritual resources by its sheer magnitude. While we may find some success
adapting to changes in one or two areas of our lives, pervasive, discontinuous change forces us to deal with changes on every front simultaneously. What's more, these changes build on each other, making it even
more difficult to know which to pay attention to and what to do next.

It's no secret that Western society has been moving through a period of radical transition for the last fifty years, but in recent years it
seems this process has accelerated. The number of changes facing us
seem to be escalating like a snowball gaining momentum as it rolls
down a hill. We no longer live in a world that provides lifetime guarantees; in fact, the only real guarantee is that unpredictable change is here

to stay. This is the new reality that is affecting not only people inside the church, but society in general. Our entire society is struggling with a volatile world filled with discontinuous change.

In his book *The Hungry Spirit*, Charles Handy calls our time "the age of unreason" and catalogues the impact of this change on our society:

> » Forty-two percent of working adults feel "used up" by the end of the day.

> » Sixty-nine percent would like to live a more relaxed life.

> » Parents spend forty percent less time with their children than they did thirty years ago.

> » Per capita consumption in the last twenty years has risen forty-five percent, while the quality of life as measured by the Index of Social Health has decreased by fifty-one percent.

> » Only twenty-one percent of young people today now think they will achieve "the good life," compared with forty-one percent twenty years ago.[4]

The days when people could expect to gradually earn more income than the previous generation—or even as they grow older—and take part in "the good life" have largely disappeared. Education and social position no longer provide guarantees that people will be better off than their parents and grandparents—particularly for the emerging generation.

Men and women are suffering in the current market place as a result of globalization and its increasing demands that people work more hours just to keep the same job. The days when people could expect to gradually earn more income and buy a stake in the good life (defined in terms of having a nice car or two, owning a home in the right suburban community, and the freedom to travel wherever and buy whatever you want) have disappeared for most members of our society.

Social theorist Ulrick Beck describes our current culture as a "risk society." In *Reflexive Modernization*, he states:

---

[4] Charles Handy, *The Hungry Spirit* (New York: Broadway, 1999), 28.

Today, people are *not* being "released" from feudal and religious transcendental certainties into the world of industrial society, but rather from industrial society into the turbulence of the global risk society. They are being expected to live with a broad variety of different, mutually contradictory, global and personal risks.[5]

In *Democracy Without Enemies*, Beck goes on to describe the long-term impact of living in this kind of environment:

Studies show that more and more people consider their life and well-being under threat . . . the general feeling of uncertainty . . . this is happening on such a massive scale that the difference between unemployment and threatening unemployment is becoming insignificant.[6]

Beck goes on to outline the transitions that have birthed this risk society.[7]

1940s – 1960s	*Rebuilding a destroyed world meshed together with the fear that what had been achieved might again collapse.* CLASSICAL VIRTUES: sacrifice, self-denial, diligence, subordination and living for others
1970s – 1980s	*Short-term dream of eternal prosperity. Earned well certain for many. Personal freedom and rights paramount. The side effects of this excess (environmental crisis, individualization), which call the foundations of primary modernity into question, were repressed.* CHANGED VIRTUES: self at the center; greed, need, identity society, self-actualization, politics of rights.
1990s – 2000s	*The 'global risk society' with a return to radical uncertainty. Trust in public and private institutions to address the crisis of late modernity are shaken and begin to disappear. People are cast adrift onto their own selves. All that can be depended upon is personal biography and a small unit of friends.*

---

[5] Ulrick Beck, Anthony Giddens, and Scott Lash, *Reflexive Modernization* (Stanford, CA: Stanford University Press, 1994), 7.

[6] Ulrick Beck, *Democracy Without Enemies* (Oxford: Polity Press, 1998), 10-11.

[7] Compare this with Robert Reich's *The Future of Success* (New York: Vintage, 2002) where he characterizes the fear ethic produced by the rapid globalization of the marketplace.

Meanwhile, British theologian Graham Ward describes our contemporary situation in terms of cultural atomism. We live in a globalized, consumerist world, he argues, where we increasingly live our lives as brief moments of experience constructed around consumerist images and events that are supposed to provide sustaining meaning:

> In this new city, the idea of distinct places is dispersed into a sea of universal placelessness . . . leading always to a single, human subject, the monadic consumer. . . . Community and social participation are telescoped into these shared emotional moments. . . . Cities are cities of the sign, concerned with image and culturally self-conscious. In the postmodern city we have moved beyond individualism with a sense of communal feeling, to a new "aesthetic paradigm" in which masses of people come together in temporary emotional communities. These are to be regarded as fluid "postmodern tribes" in which intense moments of ecstasy, empathy, and effectual immediacy are experienced.[8]

And so the question arises—what does it mean to lead communities of God in the midst of such change? No matter what form of social community one is leading, whether Liminal or Emergent, one thing is certain: it is comprised of people struggling to make sense of this new reality.

THE EFFECTS OF DISCONTINUOUS CHANGE

For Liminals, the world that formed them is passing away; for Emergents, who have little or no memory of that former world, the discontinuous change that permeates their lives makes them think that whatever they create will be better than what has been before. While Liminals remember and long for a time of stability, Emergents celebrate the shifting moments. At the same time, however, many wonder if continuity and stability can ever be found.

---

[8] Graham Ward, *Cities of God* (New York: Routledge, 2000), 59-60.

I think about a friend of mine—a young woman who recently received her Ph.D. While one might expect her to be pursuing a tenure-track position, instead she finds herself working on a contract out of three different universities in different parts of North America. She travels, writes, and does research around her own schedule, while teaching brief courses from time to time. Her list of published articles is growing and, in many ways, she would seem to be celebrating her life of change and innovation. Still, in the quiet moments, she wonders why it is so hard to form deep commitments with males her own age. She wants to live in such a relationship and have children. She wants her life to have some form of committed continuity with others, but it seems like an elusive dream. *Is it possible to be rooted and belong when so much keeps changing all the time? Is the only answer to keep relationships loose and not expect any long-term commitments?*

LEADING IN UNCERTAIN TIMES

No matter what form of social community one is leading, whether Liminal or Emergent, it is comprised of people struggling to make sense of the effects of this new society. Liminals and Emergents are responding differently to all the change around them. They are asking different questions.

Liminals ask, "How does one lead congregations, or even denominations, through this massive transition, when many want the church to return to a stable past, while others are looking for a radically alternative future?"

Emergents ask, "What skills and resources does a leader require to cultivate missional communities of Jesus in neighborhoods where people struggle to manage and survive in a confusing, turbulent 'risk society'?"

These questions are not so much about tactics and strategies as they are about our inner responses to all the changes we are experiencing. These inner responses are the real drivers of our actions and choices in the midst of change no matter what tribe we may belong to. We need to understand what they are about and where they come from if we are to effectively form missional congregations.

In his book, *The Search to Belong: Rethinking Intimacy, Community, and Small Groups,* Joseph Myers puts his finger on the questions shaping the Emergent movement:

> If there is one conversation with which the emerging church must wrestle in new ways, it is the question, "Who is my neighbor?" Who belongs? For whom am I responsible? And who is responsible for me? How can I help people develop a healthy experience of belonging and community in their lives?[9]

It's interesting to note, however, that we are not the first society to experience the impact of discontinuous change.

Our World Is Shifting

The image of a teeter-totter shifting from one side to another is an apt metaphor for Western society. There has emerged a recognizable consensus that Western society has been moving through a period of radical transition for the last fifty years and that this process of transition is continuing to pick up speed. In other words, discontinuous change is not going away.

In the fifteenth century, Europe entered a time of change just as profound, confusing, and disturbing as our own. In this period, a number of things happened to the church and its relationship to the emerging culture of what we call the "modern period."

In France, for example (and, to a lesser extent, in England), the church lost its place of power at the center of culture. It lost its control over politics, culture, intellectual life, and social morality. This change was gradual but inexorable. France became deeply secular, while England kept the symbols and forms of Christian life at the center, but emptied them of their power to determine social life.

---

[8] Joseph R. Myers, *The Search to Belong: Rethinking Intimacy, Community, and Small Groups* (Grand Rapids: Zondervan/EmergentYS, 2003), 6.

An implicit agreement was made that Christianity would vacate the public world (except when needed on special occasions by the state or academia) in exchange for being left with a kind of monopoly over the religious affections of people's private lives. This agreement lasted until recently when advances in technology and communications opened the cultures of the West to all manner of alternative, private religious options.

In North America, things worked out somewhat differently. Almost from the beginning, America established a strict separation between church and state. But in actual practice, this separation has been hard to maintain. Many of the founding stories and developing myths of the nation are so embedded with Christian symbols and images (i.e., "city on a hill," "a chosen nation," "manifest destiny," "one nation under God") that in the minds of many Americans, there is little distinction between God and country, church and nation, faith and people. While these concepts are individual, one is rarely found without the other following along hand-in-hand with the first.

America's religious history has been deeply shaped by the nation's history and social formation. Beginning with the massive suburbanization of the nation in the mid twentieth century, a deep conviction has developed (particularly among white, Protestant congregations) that individualism and economic opportunity are the highest expressions of Christian life. The gospel and Christian discipleship have been cast in terms of this larger individualistic, consumer-oriented, suburban world. Congregations have become homogenous, attracting similar people with common sets of middle-class values. While it may seem that this tendency continues to be most prominent among Liminals, in fact, both tribes can be equally self-indulgent.

For Liminals, the tendency is to work hard at attracting other Liminals—people who want a "safe" church experience where things will stay the same. Often what gets created is a ghetto of a certain socio-economic group, not an outpost of the kingdom. Emergents, meanwhile, seem to be creating gatherings of a different kind of self-focused Christians, those longing for something new. In this case, radical change becomes a sales pitch in and of itself. Those who hesitate or who cling too tenaciously to any tradition are quickly left behind.

The problem again is that both tribes have come to believe that they are alone in their struggles—that no one else is struggling with discontinuous change the way they are. And yet nothing could be further from the truth. Whether Liminals or Emergents, we are all in a new place; we are all pioneers. The name of this new place? *Transition*.

We've got to discover together how to be God's people in this strange new land. We have all, without choice or preparation, been cast into this place of transition, like it or not. As we explore how to live in this new world, we must engage both tribes in the issues of the practical nature of missional leadership. How will we develop models to deal with all of this change, while at the same time remain loyal to God's call? Can we truly become a sign, witness, and foretaste of where God is inviting all creation to Himself through Jesus Christ?

REFLECTION AND APPLICATION

1. How has discontinuous change affected your own life or that of your family in the last year? The last five years? How did you feel in the midst of that change? How did if affect your life? How would you handle that same change if it happened today?

2. Have you seen similar changes in your church in the last year? Five years? How did you and the leadership team react to them at the time? Would you handle them differently today knowing what you know now?

3. Do you see the fingerprints of this new "risk society" in what you and your church have experienced? How are these changes affecting your community?

4. How do you see this "risk society" interacting with the principles and the Gospel of the Bible? Does it make this message more or less relevant to your community and neighbors? Does something need to change then in the way your church presents that Gospel?

5. How do you see the goals of our "American dream," consumer society contrasted with the goals of the gospel of Jesus Christ? Where are they the same and where are they different? How can we nurture Jesus' call to spiritual growth and relationship to God in the midst of our missional quest to again reach our culture with God's transforming truths?

CHAPTER 3

DEVELOPING
A MODEL
FOR CHANGE

The reality is, postmodernism is not a fad... Whether or not you realize it, you live in a postmodern world... There's no point pretending you're not—or wishing that things would go back to the way they were thirty years ago. They can't; you can't....The challenge, of course, is determining what all this means for the church and knowing how to move forward.

Spencer Burke
Making Sense of Church[10]

If I am right...about the basic logic of Western Christianity since the Reformation, then at the heart of modern Christianity is a dislike of "organized religion," a distancing habit that keeps at bay the demands of a suffering intimacy with the concrete and particular forms of the apostolic witness.

R. R. Reno
In the Ruins of the Church[11]

---

[10] Spencer Burke, *Making Sense of Church* (Grand Rapids: Zondervan/EmergentYS, 2003), 26.
[11] R. R. Reno, *In the Ruins of the Church: Sustaining Faith in an Age of Diminished Christianity* (Grand Rapids: Brazos Press, 2002), 26.

Two women in their early thirties sat around our dinner table talking about their experiences with the church. One painfully described how the senior pastor of the congregation in which she was working asked her to leave because she had discussed some postmodern authors with the college-aged group. The other explained that she no longer goes to church in the old sense of a Sunday morning ritual with pews, sermons, songs, and announcements. She and some friends meet every other week at a pub where they talk theology, read the Bible, then use beer and bread as the elements of communion.

Another day I bumped into a couple who attended a church I once pastored, and they described how they're now looking for a new church. Their kids came back from summer camp wanting to attend a youth group where other campers went, so they are now trekking across town to a new church that, for the moment, fits their current list of personal needs.

These are real stories of the shifting world of church experience. Each of these people, along with the leaders of the congregations they describe, is part of a shifting environment filled with huge, open-ended questions. The word that seems to best characterize these varied experiences is *uncertainty*.

I recently visited a downtown Anglican church where my brother served on staff. The woman leading the prayer that morning asked us to pray for all those in the congregation who were facing possible job loss. Later, while driving to the airport with three other people, I realized that everyone in the car was in the midst of a job loss or major vocational change. Few Liminals expected this kind of uncertainty to dominate their lives. They started their careers expecting secure jobs to lead to secure futures, building each year on the foundations laid in previous years in a steady, linear fashion. However, this type of lifestyle has all but disappeared in today's economy.

Uncertainty is the tenor of the times—it permeates our work, our families, and the very nature of our relationships with one another. Furthermore, over the past decade or so, there has been a massive erosion of confidence in the major institutions that gave twentieth century North America its sense of stability and permanence. People's confidence in government, medicine, education, law, business, and religion as sources of trust, truth, and honesty is very low. The pillars upon which we built our social systems are now deeply suspect. In the place of confidence has emerged a broad, chronic sense of uncertainty.

At all levels, across a spectrum of roles, leaders find themselves in a strange, new, precarious location. Liminals feel this uncertainty as loss—increasing numbers of them are turning to home schooling, gated communities, or "traditional values" in efforts to fend off the uncertainty and deal with a world that feels increasingly scary. They seem to want to retreat, build walls, and defend at all costs. At the same time, many Emergents deal with the uncertainty and alienation by deconstructing our foundational institutions, including the church, hoping they can construct something more relevant to life around them from the rubble. They distance themselves from the immediate past, viewing it as unworthy of their trust. For them, it is not about where we have been, but where we might go. Their battle cry is to advance, deconstruct whatever might get in their way in the process, and hopefully discover a land of new promise just over the next horizon.

How does one name this place of uneasiness we find ourselves in today? It is the world of *transition*, and to better understand this place, I want to make a distinction between *change* and *transition*. We will deal with this distinction in more detail later, but, in brief for now, here is the distinction I would like to draw between the two:

CHANGE *is what happens to us from the outside and over which we usually have no control.*

TRANSITION *is our inner response to the changes we are experiencing and over which we do have some control.*

FRAMEWORKS FOR DIFFERENTIATING BETWEEN CHANGE AND TRANSITION

Even though the current levels of change alone are profoundly dis ruptive, they can only be understood within a larger framework. To lead congregations and denominations effectively through them leaders need to:

» Grasp the nature of this larger framework of change and transition. Without a basic grasp of their dynamics, leaders will continue feeling out-of-control and driven by tumul- tuous change into constant disorder.

» Recognize how and where change and transition are at work in the lives of the people in their churches and communities.

» Discover the appropriate images, stories, and narratives that communicate what is happening to the people among whom they live and minister.

» Connect people's experience with the biblical narratives in ways that invite them into a new understanding of what God may be up to in their world.

» Develop skills in cultivating dialogue among people about what they are experiencing in the midst of discontinuous change and how it shapes their Christian lives.

A key leadership capacity is the ability to form communities of God's people learning to dialogue together about these experiences of change and transition. In such dialogue they may hear how God desires to mold them to fit God's mission for their lives through these experiences. This requires leaders to lay aside their need to provide solutions to people's uncertainties and sense of alienation—in other words, instead of preaching and directing, leaders need to do more facilitating of dialogue and listening. As people learn to honestly take part in such dialogue with one another about the change and transition issues confronting them, they will discover ways God's Spirit addresses them through Scripture, one another, and the traditions of the church.

I think about another young couple I met who told me about their struggle to find a true church home. Their problem? One of their six children has a significant learning disability. Though they are both creative, energetic leaders, their son can be disruptive and, at times, extremely hard to manage. His disability affects his ability to socialize and build relationships. As you can imagine, the couple has gone through an agonizing process of self blame (i.e., "What did we do wrong?" "Where are we at fault?") They've attempted to balance the care of their son with the needs of their other children. They've reordered their lives in an attempt to create a healthy environment for everyone. They've struggled with doctors, medications, and even the dynamics of their own relationships with each other and their son.

And yet, throughout this time, one of the biggest challenges has been dealing with the unspoken pressures they have felt at church. The message they received was that "Christian families don't have these problems—God fixes, heals, and makes things better." Church was great at creating programs for growth or seminars on "what an ideal Christian should look like," but there was no place where people could honestly share their struggles that continually made them fall short of that ideal—no place to own and wrestle with their transitions.

The simple truth is that, unless those of us responsible for leading congregations discover a new way of nurturing growth in God's people, we may create successful congregations in terms of numbers, but miss by a million miles God's longing to mold God's people in the midst of massive, painful change and transition.

CHANGING MAPS—CHANGING FRAMEWORKS

At heart, I belong to the Liminal tribe. I grieve some of the old world that has disappeared. However, I'm also very adaptive. When my maps no longer describe the territory I live in, I try to draw new maps that better reflect the changing terrain around me. I love the challenge of the journey.

But for some people, when the map of their lives suddenly changes, the result is disorientation and confusion. We need to realize that this is not the result of some defect in them, but a normal, human response to uncertainty. When this happens we instinctively either look for ways to protect ourselves by resisting change and trying to recover what feels lost, or else we jettison our map—our past experiences—for the promise of some new, preferred future.

To give you an example of this, I want to tell you a story about my grandson. I have an intense love for my grandson. I was in the room as my daughter gave birth to him—he is our first grandchild—and since then he has become the center of my life. My greatest desire is for him to grow up with a strong sense of love and belonging while he also learns to deal with the messed up world he lives in. He has had some learning problems that doctors couldn't pinpoint even after extensive testing. The main concern is that he is behind the norm in language development. He is very bright, but his intellectual energy and imagination were being hindered because of his limitations in communicating with others. At times he would scream at his mom because he couldn't get her to understand what he wanted. The maps in his brain, which should have helped him master the communication skills he needs, were somehow not working as they should. Fortunately, all that has begun to change as he attended a school designed to work intensively with these kinds of learning problems. Ethan is now beginning to catch up with his peers in terms of language, but for a time it was hard to watch him try to communicate when the right words and thoughts wouldn't come.

When our maps of the world stop operating in the ways we expect—even though they have worked quite successfully in the past—we become confused, frustrated, and angry. This is what happens to people in the midst of discontinuous change and transition.

When we were young parents, Jane and I would read a chapter of a book out loud to our family before tucking the kids into bed for the night. The three children loved the ritual, and there was such comfort in watching them sleep in the safety of our home. This pattern of family life went on for many years until, suddenly it seemed, our eldest son turned into a teenager. The beautiful little boy shot up to over six feet, and his personality changed in ways we could never have expected—he began wearing clothes that did not fit our values and expressing beliefs and convictions that troubled us deeply. Our eldest son was tearing up the maps of a well-formed little family whose habits, patterns, and rituals were so embedded in us we believed they would last forever.

I felt confused by what was happening. Suddenly, the center of my world was out of control and nothing I did seemed to get it back into the familiar patterns. In retrospect I now realize that I acted in some fairly predictable (and really dumb) ways through those years of turmoil and discontinuity. Here are some of the basic (dumb) steps I took when my family's maps were torn up by unexpected and unwanted change.

» First, I put a tremendous amount of energy into sustaining the illusion that little of anything substantial had actually changed within our family. If we just kept doing what we'd always been doing, then sometime soon our son would return to normal and we'd all live happily ever after again. (As you might guess that didn't happen.)

» Next, I looked for any solution that would take us back to the old way of being a family. I began to emphasize the family rules and started to draw lines in the sand over what was acceptable and what would not be tolerated. I didn't want to lose my son so I worked even harder at trying to make the old rules work. (It was, of course, the worst thing I could do as the more I resisted the change, the more he resisted me!)

» Then I began to feel very incompetent and embarrassed. Other people didn't seem to have the problems we were dealing with, so what was the matter with my wife and I as parents? Where had we failed? Was I just a bad father? These inner responses and feelings (the transition being caused by these changes) only created more anxiety; I withdrew and became angry. My maps had been torn up, and I didn't have any better maps to take their place. The maps I tried using were based upon my past experience; they simply didn't work, or only managed to drive my son further away. It was a painful time.

» At some point I had to step back and ask much deeper questions about what was going on. More than anything else, I had to listen to my wife about the need to learn new skills and habits as a parent. Although it went against the grain of almost everything I had done to that point in becoming a successful adult, I knew it was time I had to change.

In both Liminal and the Emergent tribes, leaders are experiencing similar challenges—they're just as confused, scared, and pained in their struggle to lead their churches as I was to lead my family. Just as I had to stop and ask some basic questions about the frameworks that had formed me as a man and a father, leaders struggling with discontinuous change need to step back and examine the frameworks—their maps of their world—that have shaped them to this point in their journeys.

CONNECTING WITH OUR FRAMEWORKS

What are *frameworks*? They are powerful conceptual maps—or lenses—that we have developed inside our relational networks and through our training that determine how we see the world and thus shape our decisions about how to act and respond to what is happening around us.

On my street there are four pieces of property where construction workers have been digging huge holes for foundations. Once those foundations were laid, large wood frame houses began to take shape upon them. The houses were *framed*—the surrounding support structures for the house was put into place. This *framework* would define the house—or more literally, the framework would determine what was inside the house and what was outside. Once the houses are completed, we won't see these frameworks anymore—they will be covered with insulation, plasterboard, siding, paint or wallpaper, doors, windows, curtains, and all the elements that make our homes comfortable and attractive. *A framework is the underlying structure upon which we build everything else.*

If you've ever renovated a kitchen or bathroom, you know that superficial decorating doesn't solve deep down problems like water damage or termite infestation. Last year we decided to convert a solarium in our house into a new dining room for our expanding family. One task was to replace the old sliding doors with new better-insulated, higher-quality doors. As I began to remove the old doors, I discovered that, underneath all the plasterboard and cedar, the main beam holding up the roof had rotted because of the moisture from the hot tub in the solarium. Replacing the cedar wall covering or even putting in new doors would never solve this serious structural problem. The only solution was to go inside the walls, tear the old beam out, and replace it with a new one.

The picture below is of Loin's Gate Bridge, which I cross every time I travel off the North Shore into downtown Vancouver, B.C.

When I arrived in Vancouver in 1993, Loin's Gate was almost seventy-five years old, the pride of the city, a great symbol of its past—and in need of serious repair. People were increasingly afraid to cross the bridge. When I biked over the bridge I was able to see large, gapping holes in the sidewalk that revealed the ocean below. The lanes were so narrow that, at times, the side mirrors of trucks would hit other cars—it even happened to me once! Everyone knew the bridge was dangerous and, perhaps, had outlived its usefulness. If you look closely at the picture, you can see the tower and its twin cables that hold the bridge together. This is the bridge's framework. Even though the bridge is old, if this framework is repaired or replaced—in other words, brought up to a standard that meets the needs of the present—it can look forward to many more years of successful service.

Another apt metaphor that sheds light on understanding *frameworks* is a pair of glasses. When our prescription is up to date, we never think about the glasses we use to see or read. However, if the prescription becomes incorrect as our eyes grow older, we no longer see clearly.

In a similar manner, as the culture goes through major, discontinuous change, the lenses we have been using will become less and less helpful. We need new lenses to assist us in reading our context in new places of change and transition. Leaders in congregations and denominational systems are expending large amounts of energy, money, and time using products and resources for managing the complexity of our changing environment. Unfortunately, however, these systems were developed using the maps and topography of a world that is rapidly disappearing.

The following chart illustrates some aspects of the changing frameworks that will need to be developed.

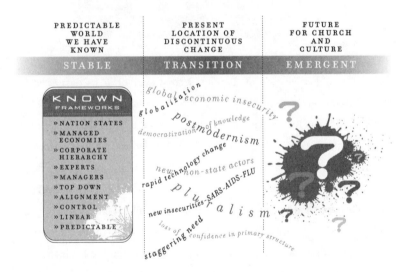

KNOWN FRAMEWORKS

The image on the left of the diagram represents some of the important frameworks that have shaped our societal assumptions of the past; these are some of the key values and commitments behind the ways we formed congregations and denominations in the twentieth century. The problem is, these are the "glasses" many leaders continue to use to try to read the new context of discontinuity and transition. As a result, most of the programs and resources offered to congregations in terms of change, process, discipleship, and leadership training come from the imagination of this old world—yet this old world has disappeared along with many of its frameworks.

Working harder at the frameworks that shaped us is a normal response to the confusion and uncertainty of discontinuous change. Author Daryl Conner says this happens in two ways. The first way is the *illusion of continuity*—people convince themselves that things remain basically the same even though much has altered. The second way is the *illusion of change*—leaders believe small modifications will satisfy the need for more fundamental change.

In both these cases the assumption is that modifying or improving one or several of the elements within one's known frameworks will effectively address the challenges of discontinuous change and transition. However, the person has done nothing to correct their basic frameworks—in other words, their "glasses" don't change. Without changing their "glasses," they become susceptible to one or both of these illusions—again, they just aren't seeing things as they truly are. Organizations who accept these illusions build a buffer between themselves and any fundamental change. Rather than making conscious, intentional responses, they accept the unconscious, natural, and, unfortunately, normal reactions to discontinuous change that provide no solutions at all.[12]

What these leaders and their organizations want to achieve is a return to the stability and equilibrium that they once experienced and thought would always be available to them. But, as Pascale, Millemann, and Gioja in their book, *Surfing the Edge of Chaos*, have pointed out, in the midst of rapid, discontinuous change, "equilibrium is death."

---

[12] Daryl R. Connor, *Leading at the Edge of Chaos* (New York: John Wiley & Sons, Inc., 1998), 12.

In their book they use the illustration of Yellowstone park

> ...where for more than a century, the park service had main-
> tained equilibrium in the forest by quickly extinguishing fires,
> denying the natural rhythm of fire and regrowth whereby
> forests cleanse and renew themselves... As a result a thicker-
> than-normal layer of deadfall and debris had built up on the
> forest floor. The 1988 lightening strikes created multiple fires.
> A prolonged drought... and ill-timed winds then conspired to
> incinerate the forest with an intensity rarely witnessed in
> North America.[13]

In the midst of massive, discontinuous change, leaders and their
organizations must learn to cultivate new frameworks, skills, and capabilities for engaging this new context of discontinuous change rather
than using the stability and equilibrium that used to be available to them.

DISCONTINUOUS CHANGE AND TRANSITION

The series of images in the center column of the diagram on page 48
represents examples of the elements contributing to our experience of
massive discontinuous change. Some are fairly obvious—pluralism,
globalization, post modernity—while others may require a deeper
analysis to recognize. Each symbolizes a movement of significant transformation that has been occurring across our culture for some years.
While each one by itself would not pose a threat to our stability and
equilibrium, in the past twenty-five years, *all of these transformations* in
our culture have come simultaneously. They have interacted with one
another, and in so doing not only changed the very nature of each other's
characteristics but also, more importantly, coalesced into a new kind of
environment that we haven't even begun to understand.[14]

---

[13] Richard Pascale, Mark Milleman, and Linda Gioja, *Surfing the Edge of Chaos* (New York: Three Rivers Press, 2000), 19-21.

[14] For more information on these transformations, see Manuel Castells, "The Information Age: Economy, Society, and Culture," in *The Emergence of the Network Society*, 2nd ed., vol. 1 (Maldon, MA: Blackwell Publishers, 2000).

All of us, Liminals and Emergents, are currently living in this unpredictable, in-between world. We are in the midst of discontinuous change and none of us are clear about what it all means. Some of us want to recover what has been lost; some of us want to jump ahead and embrace a new future we hope we can manage and control. However, many of the frameworks, skills, and abilities that worked in the twentieth century church make less and less sense in this new place. We are in the same location, perhaps from different perspectives, and we really need each other if we are going to get through this transitional time.

An Emerging Future

At this point we do not know what the shape of the future will be for either our churches or our culture. This is why the term *emergent* has caught on so widely—it signifies a future we are trying to discover even as it continues to develop. It is not predictable from the patterns of the past, nor does it look like anything we have seen before. The only thing we do know is that it is *emerging* in the midst of discontinuity and transition.

What we need, then, are frameworks, maps, skill sets, and resources for leading congregations and denominational systems in the midst of discontinuity where we cannot predict or control our futures. Yet before we can do that, we must first better understand how change happens, and thus learn to flow with it, while at the same time building the relationships that will hold us together in the midst of it, helping us discover what God is working through it.

REFLECTION AND APPLICATION

1. In your own words, describe how you would define change and transition differently. How does understanding these concepts help you in dealing with the uncertainty of the "risk society" we live in?

2. When you experience change, which are you more likely to do: go on the defensive to try to recover the past, or dump your previous maps to strike out as an explorer to uncover a new place to view everything from? Knowing this about yourself, how can you work with others in helping your church find the best way forward? What can you learn from those that have the opposite approach to our times?

3. Looking at the diagram on page 48, how would you define the terms in column one and two? How have they impacted our culture in your view? How have they impacted your community? Your church? What do you think is going to emerge from them (things that could be listed in column three)?

4. Through the discussion of frameworks in this chapter, are there ideas or concepts you have taken for granted that may need to be replaced as we face our current times of discontinuous change? What are those ideas or concepts and what do you need to replace them with to correct the prescription for your "glasses"? Is the same true for your church in the way it addresses your community and other churches in your area?

5. Read the excerpt about Yellowstone National Park on page 50 again. How does it relate to where your church is in today's society? Are there things you should "let burn" to keep from a devastating situation down the road? Are there things you should just let run their course rather than trying to control every nuance of? What changes would that require in the way your church governs itself? Are there forums or dialogues you can begin to discover these fires before they get out of control?

CHAPTER 4

THE FIVE PHASES
OF CHANGE

The shift in frameworks we need is how to imagine Christian life, congregational formation, and leadership in this world of discontinuous change. It is no longer a matter of how we get from our known world into a new world—that conversation is over! We are already living in a world drifting between the two. The questions now are: first, how do we as leaders learn to understand and function in this new world of discontinuity? And second, how do we cultivate our church structures to invite God's people to live and thrive in the midst of this uncertainty since we have no idea where it will end?

Most people in congregations today don't need to be convinced that we all live in a new kind of world, they just aren't getting any help in figuring out how to live faithfully in this crazy place. The in-between world of discontinuous change and transition discussed in the previous chapter is part of a larger process of change that has been reshaping our culture from the mid-twentieth century until today. To better understand this change, we need to identify its larger five-phase process.

The Five Phases of Change

The five phases outlined below can be found in a very brief period of time within a single organization or extremely long periods of history that move through an entire culture. The five phases are:

1) Stability (and Equilibrium)
2) Discontinuity
3) Disembedding
4) Transition
5) Reformation

These phases are illustrated in the following diagram which is presented in a figure-eight cycle:

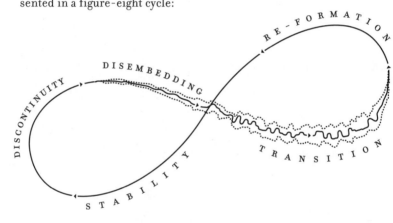

I use this irregular rotating cycle to show that the change process is not linear, but a continuous cycling in and out of periods of stability and transition. This is not to suggest any cyclical notion of history, but only to indicate that, whether in our personal, organizational, or cultural worlds, we are continually moving in and out of these phases of change. The argument of this book is that we are, culturally and as church organizations, living in the midst of transition and discontinuity. Presently, both culturally and as church organizations, we are living in the midst of discontinuity, disembedding, and transition.

However, before we discuss how these phases affect us today, let us first discuss each phase separately in greater detail.

1. STABILITY (AND EQUILIBRIUM)

> The extent to which prolonged equilibrium is a precursor of disaster must be assessed in the context of scale and time. At certain scales (i.e., small) and in some time frames (i.e., short), equilibrium can be a desirable condition. But over long intervals of time and on very large scales, equilibrium becomes hazardous. Why? Because the environment in which an organism (or organization) lives is always changing. At times, it is turbulent. Prolonged equilibrium dulls an organism's senses and saps its ability to arouse itself appropriately in the face of danger.[15]

All systems and organizations want to maintain some kind of stability. A normal response to change is the need to control the environment so that everything either finds a sense of routine equilibrium or else only changes in a linear, controlled growth pattern. Change is acceptable and manageable when it occurs inside these predictable frameworks. Discontinuous change, however, creates a crisis because it shatters these frameworks.

In a period of stability and continuity, the life of organizations and the role of leaders are highly predictable. Routines provide continuity with well-tested practices enabling organizations to operate with values and habits that have remained relatively constant for an extended period. Assumed traditions and rituals guide actions and shape the perception of reality. We see the world and read what is happening through the lenses of our organizational patterns and traditions. They connect current practices to outcomes and past expectations with strategic planning.

One example of this stability is the family. The fact is that among both Liminals and Emergents there exists a deep desire to discover, or

---

[15] Richard Pascale, Mark Milleman, and Linda Gioja, *Surfing the Edge of Chaos* (New York: Three Rivers Press, 2000), 21.

rediscover, what it means to be a successful family today. This is an example of just how disembedded we are from the traditional roles and understanding of family life. But there was, for a long time, a way of being family we considered the normal, stable form. That narrative of that family story went something like this:

> *A couple marries and has children. From childbirth to pre-adolescence, stable roles and performance expectations exist for parents and children alike. Mom and Dad will remember this period of family as a wonderful time of peace and tranquility, before the tectonic, hormonal forces of adolescence unleash themselves on the unsuspecting family.*

This period of adolescence acts as the time of discontinuity, disembedding, and transition between the stability and equilibrium of childhood, and the re-formation of the family with adult children whose parents are looking forward to the continuation of the cycle when they become grandparents.

No matter how many courses parents take, and no matter how many people have gone before, we are never ready for the incredible changes that happen with the onset of puberty. This is partly because of our tendency to believe we are different from everyone else—*we* will do it all right, or at least correct the mistakes *our parents* made. We really do believe we have the power and capacity to maintain the stability and equilibrium of family life until our children leave because we are unique. The old myth of modernity—that we can start with a clean sheet and make everything new and different—remains deep in our collective imaginations, whether it is true or not.

This period of family life when the kids are still children is like that long period in North America when the church had a relatively stable identity and role in the culture. Pastoral roles were well established and defined. While they may have been unwritten, they were still clearly understood, and had well-known rules and rituals that guided congregational and denominational life. It was a phase when congregations functioned within a broad layer of stability shaped by the power of tradition.[16]

This is not to say that organizations and leadership roles were static during this period. Tradition was continually reinventing itself as each generation, trained by the previous, assimilated the past to provide meaning to their present. Change occurred within the framework of the tradition and so was easily incorporated and accepted by its members. Also, because of continuous dialogue with the past, change was predictable, and people felt control over their environment. The world made sense and life worked because the majority subscribed to this given set of values and traditions. This phase is characterized by *evolutionary* and *developmental change*.

Evolutionary change is small, gradual, and incremental response to the exterior culture that still occurs within the assumed values of the tradition of the interior culture. Over long periods these small changes can add up to significant change. For example, Luther brought the organ into his congregations because it was the instrument university students used in the beer halls to sing their songs. Luther wanted to communicate the Gospel to these students so he brought their instrument into the church and used their music to write hymns. In response to something that was popular in the outside culture and did not violate the interior values of the church, evolutionary change occurred. Bit by bit, the organ evolved from an instrument of the pubs to one of the church culture. This is much like our introduction of the bass guitar and drums into white, middle class congregations in our time. The organ was the electric guitar of their day.

Developmental change is about improvements to already existing systems and practices. Things grow and change due to internal, not external demands. To use a family again as an example: children grow,

---

[16] For an example of this in the twentieth century church, see Coalter Milton, John Mulder and Louis Weeks, *The Organizational Revolution: Presbyterians and American Denominationalism* (Louisville, KY: Westminster/John Knox Press, 1992).

bedtimes change, conversation around the table takes on different forms, and children assume new roles with new privileges and responsibilities as they grow older. All this is an assumed part of the growth and *development* of a family or organization.

The Role of a Leader in the Stability and Equilibrium Phase.

This phase can last a long time. The values, processes, habits, traditions, roles, and norms that promote continuity are the accepted way of life. Ron Heifetz and Marty Linsky in *Leadership on the Line* state that in times of extended stability and equilibrium, the basic skills and capacities of leadership are *technical*—based upon current know-how passed on by those before them. Leadership is based on something outside of the person, such as the authority of their position in the hierarchy of the organization or the level of their education.[17]

Congregational life was formed in this environment of clear, technical leadership. Leaders were rewarded for excelling in performing the expected roles. For the first two-thirds of the twentieth century, little external stress challenged this way of life. Its assumptions formed the basis of denominational recruitment and seminary education.

The basic conduct of leadership during this time involved *management* of the status quo and the *performance* of well-established roles. High value, reward, and recognition rested on those who understood, represented, and augmented the traditions, values, and symbols of the organization. Those who questioned these values and traditions got pushed to the extremes where they couldn't disrupt the equilibrium. They were deemed threats to stability, and their words and deeds were interpreted as undermining tradition. The system neutralized such people in order to maintain stability.

This is the world for which the Liminals were trained and in which they thrive. However, when discontinuous change becomes the norm rather than stability, they are thrown into disarray. For them it is like

---

[17] Ronald A. Heifetz and Marty Linsky, *Leadership on the Line: Staying Alive Through the Dangers of Leading* (Harvard: Harvard Business School Press, 2002), 14.

walking into a room of nuts and bolts with only a screwdriver. Their tools no longer fit their environment. In response to seeing this, some call for jettisoning all tools and hoping to come up with some better solution to dealing with their times—these are the Emergents. Their shortcoming is that it is not something besides tools that they need, but rather different tools. But they are unlikely to make this discovery without going back to understand what has happened before.

2. DISCONTINUITY

Periods of stability cannot last forever. Sooner or later, patterns of change slowly begin to emerge that will profoundly alter the way the world works. History is filled with examples of this. Again, this is like the period in the family when children enter adolescence: they begin to search for their own identity, challenging previously assumed values and beliefs. Parents either become highly adaptive or full-scale rebellion and family rift ensue.

Congregations and denominational systems entered this phase of change in the last quarter of the twentieth century when powerful but amorphous forms of change began pushing back on accepted traditions and *institutional* structures. Even while the church seemed to be doing well in America, a continual, growing restlessness was birthing the emergence of groups challenging the fixedness of its traditional forms, the accepted roles of leaders, and the stability of its existence. Underlying this emerging discontinuity was a sense that the churches were failing to engage the massive changes sweeping through American culture. As a result, many broke away from the traditional in search of new forms of what "church" should look like.

Today we experience this as the continued clash between the churches shaped by the Liminals (those who stayed) and those being formed by the Emergents (those who broke away). Again, it is not unlike the struggle between parent and adolescent. Successful Liminals in very large congregational networks wanted to gather the younger Emergents together to discover key transferable concepts they could take from mega-boomer, seeker-oriented traditional churches and apply them to the new generation of Emergents. Leaders in the Emergent tribe reacted to this as a plan to pour them back into the Liminal mold and never came to the meetings.

This tension continues. Within congregations and across denominations, there exists a huge amount of fluctuation as people shift back and forth between churches looking for the styles, programs, and values that best meet their personal needs. This new religious environment is spirituality *à la carte*. The seekers just take a little from here and a little from there until their plates are full and never bother to see if the different things they have taken complement each other—one may have all desserts, and another all breads, but they don't seem to care just as long as their plates are full.

Increasingly, through the Internet (web sites, blogs, chat rooms, etc.), books, and conferences, growing numbers discover alternative narratives and ways for forming church life in just this fashion. Of course, they then expect change from their leadership, which creates tension. Leaders are relatively unskilled at negotiating challenges to established patterns and assumptions. Liminals feel deeply threatened. Emergents tend toward accepting all kinds of experimentation without an understanding of the dynamics of change within existing systems.

In each case, leaders become hurt and confused. Long-practiced traditions and values are called into question. A context of increasing stress is created as some struggle to mediate changing relationships, others fight to maintain their traditions, and still others try to pull everything apart so that they can start from scratch.

The Role of a Leader in the Discontinuity Phase. In this phase leadership doesn't change from the previous phase, but remains based in *management, performance* of established roles, and *technical* skills. There is little understanding of the dynamics of the discontinuous change rattling the system. The emphasis is upon simply trying to improve or augment what has worked before. Frameworks are not questioned, though the need for flexibility within them begins to dawn on many. However, the overriding belief is that current methods of dealing with change and conflict will still work. The leader's comfort zone is in *performing* the same role he or she always has and in continuing to apply the *technical* skills in which he or she was trained. As a result, these leaders are running faster and working harder while also falling further behind the curve of change. They grow tired and discouraged, but don't know what else to do.

Leaders usually can't imagine a future other than simply managing small evolutionary and developmental changes within their organization. The tendency is to try to negotiate relationships back to stability. The reality is that the dynamics of change in this phase are now moving at such a rate that leaders are missing the actual issues of change that need addressing. Managing the challenges sweeping over denominations and congregations from the perspective of tradition and stability marginalizes the capacity to lead an organization. Yet, in this second phase, the basic orientation of leadership remains directed toward the *maintenance of tradition*. The result is that leaders and their organizations experience growing levels of stress and confusion as *role-performance* and *technical* forms of management become less and less congruent with the realities.

3. DISEMBEDDING

Discontinuity increases until the power of the tradition that was so crucial in the stability phase can no longer function as the glue to hold the system together. Internal and external pressures are becoming too great to simply maintain and manage what-has-been. At this point stress is everywhere—relationships are strained, and the system begins to break apart.

This is seen in denominational organizations as their congregations opt to join new networks or groups whose primary purposes seem to be reshaping identity. One denominational leader expressed the predicament of leadership in this change well when he told me that the congregations in his system no longer looked to him for expertise and advice, but were instead turning to sources within other networks. He and his associate are now trying to figure out what these networks are offering and if they can work with them so they can get back to helping their own congregations! This is a massive shift of leadership roles and imagination.

Congregations are rapidly disembedding themselves from former relationships within denominational systems and leaders are running to catch up with little time to reflect on what it all might mean in terms of key change issues. At this point, the role of leadership becomes primarily *reactive* in nature.

Power struggles emerge within these organizations, especially where congregations or denominations lose significant amounts of their financial base. In these cases people will fight over who gets the diminishing dollars or whose staff and programs will experience the deepest cuts. Conflicts and blame-shifting are common.

This process of *disembedding* is the uprooting of deeply connected relationships, beliefs, practices, and values. It is very stressful; but it is also necessary.

Furthermore, this disembedding is not only local, but it is also cultural. The Western church is being systematically disembedded from its long-established place at the center of culture, while at the same time it is being increasingly disembedded from its own inner story as it struggles with a growing number of attempts to restate its story in ways that make sense of larger cultural shifts.[18]

The combination of both local and cultural disembedding processes is proving to be very difficult for leaders at this moment. When tra-

---

[18] See, for example, Brian McLaren's *A New Kind of Christian* and *The Stories We Find Ourselves In*; R.R. Reno's *In the Ruins of the Church*; and Darrel Guder and Lois Barrett's *Missional Church* as examples of this process.

ditional relationships disconnect, when habits and ways of operating change, when all kinds of new experiments emerge and once cohesive groups begin to tribalize around issues, then the entire way of life for the church is rapidly approaching an advanced state of erosion.

Several further observations about this phase need to be noted. The essential drive of modernity is to erase and disconnect all things from the past unless they contribute to its own agenda for the future. The critical turn of mind—observe Descartes' famous dictum: *cogito ergo sum:* "I think, therefore I am," indicating that individual cognition is the source of being human, not any relationship to external standards, institutions, or being(s)—denies tradition, or any other external source, the authority to determine or shape action. Modernity is based upon a fundamental presupposition of discontinuity and disembedding from past tradition and any authority other than the self's autonomous reason.

There are at least two critical results to this. First came a three-hundred-year period of change unparalleled by any other in human history. These changes have been so dramatic, so comprehensive, and so pervasive that we are still struggling to work through their impact on our lives and social systems. Second, most of this change has occurred without reference to tradition or the past. As a result, this disembedding has created a sense of disorientation for many people, a sense of being caught in a whirl of change that they don't understand and is beyond their control. We are sailing in the deeply unsettling waters of this radical disembedding of all the social institutions formed over the past several centuries.[19]

The Role of a Leader in the Disembedding Phase. In this third phase, leadership—as manager, counselor, or the chaplain of *role-performance* and *technical* skills—will not enable a meaningful engagement with the new social context. A different kind of response is required. This presents a huge challenge as leaders are caught in change they

---

[19] See the writings of Ulrick Beck et al. *(Reflexive Modernization)* and Zygmunt Bauman *(In Search of Politics)* for helpful analysis of this disembedding across Western societies.

never anticipated. Leaders now require *adaptive* skills to anticipate, create, and revise their institutional cultures. The pastoral skills in which they were trained are important, but no longer sufficient to handle all they will face.

In discontinuity and disembedding, changes keep coming like a long series of quakes and aftershocks. The expectation is that they will eventually settle down, or go away, and a stable period will return. Thus, the basic orientation of leaders is to struggle through until the system returns to balance. Yet this will not happen. The shocks and quakes will keep coming—there will be no end to the surprises.

4. TRANSITION

This is the most difficult phase. Stability, predictability, and control within a former world are long gone. The traditions of the past framework have now been disembedded from the culture. Expectations and perceptions of how things ought to work have less and less correlation with what is, in fact, happening. Contrary to expectation, the churning of change has not led to a new period of stability. There is little clarity about what is happening and a lot of confusion about what to do.

This phase is about the realities of a loss of road signs and mile markers. The natural instincts are still to find places of stability and equilibrium, but they are nowhere to be found. The need for control and predictability still assert themselves in powerful ways. Oddly enough, congregations and organizations that promise people a return to stability will thrive in this period, even though they can't truly provide it. Since everyone is looking for stability, when these churches say they can provide it, people flock to them like moths to a flame. Then, to make it worse, the promise seems validated because certain types of congregations do thrive (and they are generally homogeneous, middle-class, and suburban). Other leaders then see them as signs of hope and choose to copy their tactics, though doing so only pushes them even farther from embracing the transition around them and honestly addressing its demands.

At a recent conference focused on church growth and seeker-directed leadership, a Mennonite pastor walked into an elevator I was using. Bemused by the discrepancy between the theological and ecclesial imagination of Mennonites and the nature of the conference, I asked him why a Mennonite was at such an event. His response was quick and direct: "Because it works!" In the midst of massive discontinuity, disembedding, and transition, leaders desire to find something that "works" rather than stopping long enough to understand what is actually happening.

People look for what works in order to find a way back to the prior period of stability and tradition. Like the shipwrecked Robinson Crusoe, the first thing we do is try to build a boat to try to get back to life that was lost. Crusoe used what had worked before the island, but soon learned that he had to discover new skills to function in the radically new place. The church in North America is in this same position.

At the beginning of this phase, the stress created by the loss of control over one's environment is high. Leaders have a variety of responses. They seek external resources that promise ways of reinstating control without changing the substantive nature of the system. But the primary goal is to maintain the inner integrity of their framework. There is generally little thought put into the question of fundamentally reinventing the system itself.

In contrast, however, this is also a time of immense opportunity. The potential for something new to emerge is great. It is this phase where most congregations and denominations find themselves today. While it is highly stressful, it is also a phase that must be *lived in* for some time if we are to discover the kinds of futures God may want to call forth for God's church.

5 . REFORMATION

Reformation happens as the church has negotiated the reinventing of its life through discontinuity, disembedding, and transition, and begins to approach a new period of recreating tradition and finding fresh stability. In this time the church's original story is being reframed in new structures, roles, and expectations. Here the sustaining, underlying narrative of Christian life has been reappropriated; but such reappropriation has occurred in such a way that all frameworks around the story have changed radically. A new language, a new set of roles, and a new set of rules have emerged to reveal structures and ways of living that bear little resemblance to the previous period of stability.

Unfortunately, I don't believe we are anywhere near this period in the life of North American churches. We are merely at the beginning of the fourth phase: transition. The kind of churches that will emerge through these last two phases remains an open question and will remain so for years to come.

LEARNING TO WORK WITHIN DISCONTINUOUS CHANGE

As the figure-eight diagram on page 54 suggests, the movement through these phases is not linear. Furthermore, to interpret this process too literally is to oversimplify it and misses its nuances. Nothing is ever that neat and tidy.

The usefulness of the model is that it helps us to a) locate ourselves, our culture, and our church systems within the overall flow of a complex process of change, and b) give a common language to what is happening to us so we can come together to discuss it. This naming of where we are now is critical to moving forward on this journey of change.

The phases are not cut-and-dry. The shift from one phase to another occurs over extended periods of time. There are periods between each phase that are, themselves, transition zones when the previous phase is being subordinated to the emerging phase. All the elements of the earlier phase aren't simply discarded and forgotten, but remain as a memory of habits with the power to affect the current phase. This is why it is essential to see where we are in the overall change process rather than simply concentrating on the immediate phase and believing that is all there is and all there ever will be.

Movement through phases is never a smooth, uniform progression. It is a difficult, uncertain, confusing, stop-and-go, back-and-forth process. This was the character of change throughout the last half of the twentieth century as the disconnecting processes within modernity and Christianity accelerated. The movement of change from a stable, functional Christendom to its present loss of centrality to our culture has been going on for at least the past three hundred years. As we enter the next shift, times become increasingly more traumatic and difficult.

The shift from transition into reformation is still a long way ahead of us. The reforming phase will be shaped by how we adapt and change in this phase of transition. The shift will probably take two or three generations. Here is where Liminals and Emergents will need each other in the coming years. The processes of change we're all involved in is more than a battle between two groups over style or generational difference.

We are all in the early stages of a massive transition. Both Liminals and Emergents bring key insights and values to this place. We need to find a common ground in the midst of a time when none of us will find clear answers or complete solutions. We cannot return to the past like some nostalgic *That 70s Show*, nor jump over the present to go bravely where none have gone before like some kind of *Star Trek* series. We are more like the strange, motley crew of creatures struggling to make sense of their situation on board the space station *Babylon Five*. We know that a way of life is over and a world has passed away, but we are also disturbingly aware that no one knows what the future is going to look like. We must discover new ways of being together in this place.

In summary I would note four principles:

1) Change at a particular moment must be understood as part of the phases, not in isolation.

2) In the *stable* phase, the primary skills are *technical* involving the *management* and *performance* of

received or inherited traditions and frameworks. Classical pastoral training is shaped by this period. Change is *evolutionary* and *developmental*.

3) Beyond the first phase something more than management is required. *Adaptive leadership* must become primary rather than focusing on *technical*, *role-performance*, and *management* skills.

4) Leadership will require living in the midst of the tension between reentering the stories and traditions of our past *and* experimenting in ways that discern the *emergent* forms of God's activity. Both Liminals and Emergents need each other to help them in this process.

The present location of both North American culture and the church is *transition*. Before looking at the skills and capacities leaders will need for this context we must next look at where our primary Christian narrative in Scripture informs this discussion.

Reflection and Application

1. Take a minute and write out or discuss with your group what you feel would be a good job description of a pastor for a congregation such as yours. Which of the items in this list do you see applying directly to a time of stability and equilibrium? What characteristics on your list would you label as managing skills? Which are technical skills? Is there anything on your list that doesn't fit under either category? Are there other skills and abilities that you feel would need to be added to this for the time of transition we are in now?

2. In your own words, describe the five phases of change listed in this chapter and then give examples of each from your community and church. What leadership attributes do you see most positively affecting each of these periods of time?

3. What skills and abilities would you make for the job description of an adaptive leader? Which do you feel you are the strongest at in leading your congregation? Which are your weakest? Where can you look to find individuals who are strong in your weaknesses and can help you lead your congregation in this time of transition?

4. List some examples of evolutionary and developmental change your church has gone through in the last few years. What have been the results of these changes? Have they helped or do you see them falling short of the types of fundamental changes that really need to happen?

5. Take some time to think about how your framework has started to change as you have read this book. What has been the most helpful so far? What others in your church or community would you most like to discuss these issues and ideas with?

DISCONTINUOUS CHANGE: THE BIBLICAL NARRATIVE

Judah mourns
    and her gates languish;
[her people] *lie in gloom on the ground,*
and the cry of Jerusalem goes up.

Her nobles send their servants for water;
    they come to the cisterns,
they find no water,
    they return with their vessels empty.

                    Jeremiah 14:2-3 [insert added]

The imagination for living as God's people in our time comes from two places: first, the biblical narratives that form the fundamental story of Christian life; and second, the concrete realities of living in the midst of today's church. The one cannot be separated from the other. Each is critical for the development of an imaginative engagement with our context. Because of this, I would like to take some time at this point to address the concrete reality of the churches out of the biblical narratives.

This is not about trying to recapture some past moment, but neither is it about trying to define some radical future. Neither option takes the church seriously as it is. Both want, in their different ways, to deny the present fact of the church as it finds itself lying in confusion amidst North American culture. The cisterns are empty and there is no water, despite any contemporary Hananiah promising that in just a short time everything will be right again. Hope for the church is not found in methods of retaking the culture and remaking Christian life, nor in adapting the church to match some form of postmodern life; it is found in a readiness to live *in the midst of a church that languishes* where there are few answers but the possibility of again hearing God's word as it directly addresses us today. The book of Jeremiah addresses just such a time of transition as the one we live in and offers rich resources for discerning the ways we can engage our time of discontinuity and change.

Despite our apprehensions and confusion, the church can learn to live and thrive in the midst of this transition period. Biblical narratives such as Jeremiah provide a way of hope that will seem counterintuitive. When I present this material in conferences, people respond very differently. Some react sharply; they can see no hope in what is being described because no tactics are presented to manage and control outcomes for some preferred future. Others embrace the picture being presented, but want to know how to lead in a context where there can be no answers in terms we are comfortable with from our familiar frameworks.

The story of God's engagement with Judah in Jeremiah addresses both of these issues. Jeremiah addresses both the Liminal and Emergent tribes. While we will examine it in some detail in a later chapter, what I would like to share here is a brief summary of the ways that the biblical narrative illustrates the five phases of change we have previously outlined.

STABILITY: LIVING AS COVENANT PARTNERS

Massive discontinuous changes, on scales larger than we are currently experiencing, were always part of Israel's history. Our particular moment is part of the ongoing narrative of God's passionate, relentless encounters with those shaped by the biblical story. The dislocations and discontinuities reshaping the church are not independent of God's purposes or activities. Just as they were for Judah, they are part of the dynamic ways God encounters our lives today.

The Old Testament narratives comprise an overarching account of God's engagement with God's people for the sake of the world. This was a hard relationship that required the remaking of these people in ways they could never have imagined. Over the course of Israel's life up to the birth of Jesus, we can identify many examples of the five phases of change at work. Take, for example, their story after entering the land with Joshua.

Israel enters the land, conquers many of the other tribes already present and chooses to live as God's covenant partner within a loose tribal confederacy that has no central government. *Yahweh* is their protector, giving them a particular identity and way of life that differentiated them from all the other peoples of the earth. In the land, Israel began to settle into a way of life radically different from who they were as wandering tribes in the backside of the desert, or even as slaves in Egypt.

God intended the relationship framed in desert living and covenant commitment to be the basis for their way of life in the new land. This involved living under God's protection and not that of a king, as all the nations that surrounded them did. Their relationship with God was to be primary and concrete; Israel was to be a distinct people, an expression of a culture and society shaped by their covenant relationship with God. When Israel entered the Promised Land, they understood themselves as a people shaped by the powerful events of the Exodus and entrusted with a mission for the sake of the world. Unfortunately, this traditional identity did not hold for very long.

DISCONTINUITY: COVENANT LIFE ABSORBED AND SUBSUMED

Other tribes in the land and great nations in the area brought pressure on the Israelite confederacy. Their theocracy became uncomfortable for them, and the people began to cry for a reshaping of their national identity into a monarchy. The elders and those rooted in the ancient traditions resisted this demand for change. A series of charismatic judges were offered as alternatives to a king. For a time this answered the people's concerns, but the forces of change continued to press upon the loose clans of Israel.

DISEMBEDDING: CRISIS AND CHAOS

The Israelites began to enter into treaties and commercial relationships with the surrounding groups in order to ward off conflict; as well as guarantee their own place of economic and political control. In so doing, they rewrote the meaning and images of the covenant. Its primary demands were gradually subsumed and absorbed into the larger culture. False images of God and covenant relationship led to false images of their own identity and purpose in the world. Eventually this world was shattered by invasion and exile.

A crisis of massive proportions ensued. Nebuchadnezzar invaded the land, destroyed the temple, leveled the walls of Jerusalem, and transported the best and brightest of Judah into exile in Babylon. Because of their warped sense of covenant, it is an unimaginable event. Despite the warnings of prophets, the people had no framework to understand, accept, or receive the catastrophic events of 587 B.C. This was not only a crisis of politics, but also of faith and identity. It was the loss and ending of a world—resulting in complete disorientation and chaos. This cataclysmic event was a total shock.

The people were transferred to a radically new, alien, threatening world. As Psalm 137:4 cries out, *"How could we sing the LORD's song in a foreign land?"* This was no rhetorical question. It was the anguished cry of a confused people who had lost their world. They were living in the midst of grief, pain, and a bottomless anger at their sense of desertion and abandonment. The alignment of God's kingdom with the values and practices of the dominant culture had left Israel blind to what was actually going on.

TRANSITION: REDISCOVERING GOD

The Babylonian Exile meant Judah was disembedded from Jerusalem. The Hebrews did not know how to live or think about God in this strange, alien place. But in the midst of and because of the trauma and chaos of exile, they began to rediscover their most fundamental narratives about themselves as a people, their vocation, and the nature of the God who had called them to uniqueness. This involved reentering their primary stories and traditions from a radically new perspective. It was not handed down from the mountaintop in power and authority, but emerged from their sense of loss and confusion as they returned to the Scriptures looking for answers. Only in this ambiguous location did they discern both the nature of God and the possible future God intended for them.

Exile became the place where the people painfully relinquished the dreams of old Jerusalem. This would not be instantaneous, but would take several generations. Furthermore, in this process of relinquishment, Israel would also have to spend many years rediscovering God's story and their traditions. These had been subverted and lost in the long acclimation with the surrounding cultures of their land.

In the biblical accounts, exile was a hopeful moment in Israel's life. Hosea used the metaphor of the desert and exile as a symbol of God acting like a lover, intent upon wooing and winning back a love that had turned to others for solace and satisfaction. Exile is a symbol of God's gracious preparation, not God's abandonment! Babylon was the place in which Israelites had to fundamentally rethink their understanding of God and the tradition they had taken for granted. Only out of this long process would a new imagination—a new identity as God's people— begin to emerge. The Babylonian Exile was Israel's period of transition.

REFORMATION: RETURNING HOME

Following seventy years of exile (almost three generations), a generation emerged that was shaped by the exile and the process of recovering covenant memory. Ezra and Nehemiah began to express the hope of a return to Jerusalem to rebuild its walls and recreate the temple. Although they attempted to return to the normalcy of the past, they found that it could not be recreated—too much has changed. There was too much instability.

Israel was located at the crossroads of history—they lived on the trampling grounds of empires. Their dreams of God's future involved the expectation of recapturing from their past. The dynasty of David becomes the mirror with which they looked over their shoulders to imagine God's future. It is only in the Diaspora communities that genuinely new forms of life would emerge.

These stories of return are accounts of a people struggling through transition toward a different future. The passion was for restoration (back to the future). While some of this was essential (for example, the walls needed to be rebuilt) and required remembering their history, traditions, and older skills, this was not the only form of imagination that returned from the exile.

TODAY'S PLACE OF TRANSITION

Cultures, organizations, and individuals move through never-ending processes of formation, acculturation, crisis, transition, and rebirth. This was the ongoing reality for Israel. In the same way there is something going on in our own time—it is a new epoch. Despite this, we know that it is neither new nor unique in terms of God's purposes. It has already been encountered repeatedly in the history of Israel in her relationship with God.

In many ways, the church today is in a similar phase of transition Judah faced in Babylon. While this place is full of great challenges and threats, it is also full of great opportunity for those who will seek to listen and understand. If we are going to transform our churches we will need to understand the threats and embrace the opportunities presented by our time of transition. We must come to grips with this concept of *Liminality*.

Reflection and Application

1. What parallels of the Babylonian Exile do you see for Christianity in today's society? In what ways is our situation similar? In what ways is it different? In what ways does this metaphor contribute to seeing ourselves as missional in our own culture?

2. Can you think of other stories in the biblical narrative that exemplify the five phases of change? What are they? (We will look at some more examples of these in chapter eight.) Can you think of historical examples that also illustrate them? Share examples of each.

3. Are there things we have taken for granted as God's people that are possibly being uprooted in our culture today, just as Judah's sense of divine protection was contradicted by going into exile? How do you see these things changing in the times ahead?

4. What promise do you see for us to return to the biblical narrative for answers as Judah did? What do you feel are some of the best ways we could do this? What parts of the Bible do you think would be most helpful for us to study with this hope in mind?

5. What do you see as the threats and opportunities we face today in our time of transition? How are they similar to and different from what Judah faced in Babylon? What do you think are some of the best ways we can face the threats and embrace the opportunities?

LIMINALITY—
THE CHARACTER
OF TRANSITION

I n a scene from the television series *West Wing*, the President and his aides are in the early stages of planning for the second-term elections. Powerful lobby groups are vying for attention and presenting their demands in return for support of the President's reelection.

One businessman sitting in the Oval Office makes it clear the President must sign legislation making it possible to offshore software design jobs to Asia. This policy, he argues, will guarantee competitiveness in a global market; a decade from now it will result in thousands of new, high tech jobs for Americans. The President wants to know how many jobs will be lost in the short term as a result of the legislation. "Perhaps ten thousand, no more," is the response. They agreed.

Later, a presidential aide stood in the Oval Office arguing against the decision because the President had promised unions during the first election campaign that their jobs would be protected. Although the President acknowledged this, he argued that he had no control over globalization; he could only try to ameliorate its impact on American lives. The idealistic aide countered with the importance of keeping one's word, to which the President responded with a lecture on the realities of political decisions and restated his commitment to the ordinary worker. Even though the decision would be tough on some people, it would also result in more new jobs in the long run. For now, the government had to provide transition-training funding for workers who would lose their jobs. He then told the aide to meet with union leaders to convince them this was the best decision, given the unpredictability of change in the globalized world.

In the next scene, the aide sat in his office with a union leader and two workers—a man and a woman—who would be affected by the policy change. The union leader didn't argue or use power politics; he simply introduced the man and woman with him—both computer programmers who would lose their jobs. He then explained that the job losses would be more like thirty thousand than ten thousand. With that, he left the two workers in the room with the aide.

The woman, in her late twenties, expressed her consternation at the fact that getting a university degree in computer engineering did not protect her from the off-shoring of high tech jobs. The aide, feeling her struggle, explained that the government would provide several millions of dollars for job retraining so that she, and others like her, could retool for a new job market.

The man, in his mid-forties, described his situation—with two kids in college, as a father, he had expenses that couldn't be matched by job retraining programs. He explained, "I have a good university degree, and at this point in my life I expected to be in a secure job that provides for my family. You tell me I can retrain and redirect my skills. It's the second time this has happened to me! I've already been through one of your job retraining programs and shifted into computer programming because it was supposed to be one of those high tech jobs that would always be here. How many more times can a man in his mid-forties with a family and bills retrain?"

The aide had no answer. The room was silent.

This is the world of *transition*.

At a conference with young leaders from churches and denominations across North America, a speaker presented a theological description of the new *missional ecclesiology*. Basically, the message was that times have changed and we can no longer continue shaping congregations and denominations as if nothing has happened. There is talk about experiments and the need for a new kind of church, or even a new kind of Christian. These young leaders were told that the forms of leadership that have functioned in the church for such a long time are now deficient—they've become liabilities to the formation of the church we must become. But when they ask what this church might look like or what forms of leadership will be required, the response was vague generalizations filled with comments such as: "We don't have answers. It's all got to emerge."

This may be honest and truthful, but it leaves younger leaders hanging in midair with no practical sense of what to do next. They now know what they don't want and what needs to be left behind, but there is little sense of what they do need and should want in the present.

They are also in the tough world of *transition*.

I received an e-mail from a pastor recently who wrote:

> I am part of a church community that understands the need for missional change. As a leader of a year-and-a-half, I have intuitively refused to continue the pattern of strategic planning, programming, and objectifying the "can'ts" as part of the machine. This was "successful" in this church in the past and so becomes a default position. As we are becoming more and more missional, we are struggling with how to lead (often to the sounds of "Why won't you lead!"). I have recognized, to some degree, what we bought into and called the "church." I have not wanted to be part of this. . . . One of the most difficult weights I carry right now is how to be a leader in what I call a "chaotic" church. I have trained

> for what is passing and has passed and I know it. As
> nice as it would be to find myself comfortable again (or
> at least not quite as mystified all the time), I know I
> cannot personally turn back.

This pastor is also in *transition*—this world of discontinuous change. We can see where we've come from, and we know we're in a very different place now, but the question everyone's asking is: "How do we function here?" Transition is a world with few maps. It's a time of great opportunity and great temptation. We deal with it in different ways depending on our background, experience, and, to some extent, our stage in life.

LIMINALS AND EMERGENTS IN TRANSITION

Liminals and Emergents deal with this transition period differently. Liminals generally find it scary—how do you keep retraining for uncertain futures when you're in your mid-forties, your kids are in college, the bills are piling up, and there's now no pension on the horizon? The familiar geography keeps changing and the predictable maps keep shifting.

How does one start over again with new rules right in the middle of the game? How will the pastor—after twenty years of experience leading the church in a certain way using strategic planning and programs— learn new skills and develop new capacities in the midst of a congregation filled with similar anxieties and who demand that he fix their world and remove their anxieties? How does a Liminal retool for this *postmodern* context that he neither understands nor, if the truth were known, appreciates? He is in a stage of life when, by right, he and other leaders like him should be at the top of their game—yet, instead, they are discovering that they have to learn to play the game all over again. Few are prepared for this!

For Emergents, the issues are different, but the questions are the same. They are often exhilarated by the discontinuities in which we are living. In one's twenties and thirties, change is like a drug—it energizes and excites because the world is there for the remaking. It's not difficult to navigate change—our baggage is light, so we can pick up and move on quickly. All of life lies ahead of them and they can't wait to get there.

But is it that simple? A majority of young leaders I've encountered feel adrift with a sense that they have few, if any, mentors who have gone ahead and can guide them along a safe path. This creates its own kind of anxieties, because so many of their experiments fail, resulting in all kinds of personal and relational uncertainties. Lots of Emergent leaders are trying their experiments without the wisdom and maturity of others who have been down the same path and who understand the implications of what they are doing and who have the skills needed. Experimentation and not being prejudiced by the past can be wonderfully serendipitous values in the abstract, but in the hard reality of working with real people in real organizations, the results can be that they are like ships without earth anchors or compasses.

But there is still more to it than that. The current levels of cultural disruption moving through our society are high. The reality of living without maps and markers is quite destructive for Liminals and Emergents alike.

A recent *New York Times* article described how the age when sexual activity begins is getting younger and younger. Today, children ages 10-11 are becoming sexually active. The ways they are doing this is also very scary. One group of kids interviewed described their sexual relationships as having "friends with benefits." By this they mean that they can have sex without the pressures of any commitment to be girlfriend/boyfriend. They can get together to have sex and then play video games together afterwards. It is all one seamless whole—each is just a different way of "playing" together. Sex is just another activity friends can do together! However, the consequences of the sexual intimacy is still the same no matter what they claim—both physically and emotionally. They are just trying harder and harder to pretend that they aren't.[20]

Another case told of teenagers getting together for "rainbow parties." Individual girls in a group will each wear different colors of lipstick, then have oral sex with each of the boys at the party, who get bragging rights based on the assortment of colors they wear. The deception is that they are told this is a normal part of socialization—it's not *sex*, and it is not intimate and binding, it's just a game.[21]

These young people live in a world that has lost its maps. No wonder Oprah and Dr. Phil are so incredibly popular—they have become the new cultural authorities on social and moral standards for generations that have emerged into a world without signposts and mile markers to direct their journeys.

It is not sufficient to simply experiment and then move on to other experiments. This only postpones the inevitable creation of new sets of confusion and pain to somewhere down the road instead of honestly facing them today. We still need mentors and guides. We still need those who have wisdom for the journey ahead. The difficulty of this moment is that such people are very hard to find. The best way to counter this difficulty is for the Emergents to reconnect with the Liminals and start talking these issues through—only then can leaders emerge that have a solid perspective of where we have been and the best roads ahead to take us where God wants us to go.

The book *The Church in the Emerging Culture* describes this transition time as both a world of a disembedded and changing modernity and an emerging postmodern culture. Len Sweet comments:

> We find our brainpower drained by issues of boundaries and allegiances during this transition time:

[20] Ann Brashares. *"Under the Covers,"* New York Times, Sunday, July 31, 2005. Section 4. Page 13f
[21] Ibid.

> Which culture do we belong to or react against or with-
> draw from or seek to transform? The dominant-but-
> fading modern culture or the fledgling, emergent,
> divergent postmodern ones? To speak of Christian
> identity and the identity-culture dilemma in the midst
> of seemingly parallel cultural universes is to press one
> of the hottest buttons in the church today.[22]

The fact that this is a hot button issue may be a factor of the way the conversation is set up as if the Emergents and the Liminals are on opposing
sides, as if there is a polarity that compels people to choose sides.
Polarities are to be managed, not turned into an either/or choice. It is in
the ability to live in the midst of the polarity that the creative life of a
people and a time is discovered.

The Time in Which We Lead

Walter Brueggemann describes our time as one in which an old
imagined world is lost, although still powerfully cherished. It is a time
of bewilderment and fear because there's no clear understanding of how
to order our common imagination differently or better. He states:

> I believe we are in a season of transition, when we are
> watching the collapse of the world as we have known it
> . . . the value systems and the shapes of knowledge
> through which we have controlled life are now in great
> jeopardy. One can paint the picture in very large
> scope, but the issues do not present themselves to
> pastors as global issues. They appear as local, even
> personal, issues, but they are nonetheless pieces of a
> very large picture. When the fear and anger are imme-
> diate and acute, we do not stop to notice how much of
> our own crisis is a part of the larger one, but it is.[23]

Brueggemann describes this transition as a troubling place to dwell, but
it is exactly where we must dwell. There is no other time or place to
which God has called us to live but this one.

---

[22] Leonard Sweet, ed., *The Church in Emerging Culture* (Grand Rapids: Zondervan/Emergent YS, 2003).
[23] Walter Brueggemann, *Hopeful Imagination* (Philadelphia: Fortress Press, 1986), 45-46.

Sister Mary Jo Leddy describes it as a period when the great tapestry of religious life woven in North America over several hundred years has unraveled and lies in tatters on the floor of our culture. She explains:

> We are living through one of those historical in-between times when a former model of religious life (either traditional or liberal) is fading away and a future model has not yet become clear. One could be tempted to flee from the dilemmas of this moment to some more secure past, to the surface of the present, or to some arbitrary resolution of the future. These are real temptations and they can be met only with the faith that this is our hour, our *kairos* [Greek for "season" or "time"]. This is the only time and place we are called to become followers of Jesus Christ; there is no better time or place for us to live out the mysteries of creation, incarnation, and redemption. These are our times and, in the end, God's time.[24]

This is our time. It is not a place for simplistic, dualistic, us-versus-them thinking. We have not left modernity behind, but we are in a place that seems so unlike the ethos, experiences, values, and attitudes of the last half of the twentieth century. The generations that led in that era are passing, but there are still many "emerging-age" leaders who work with all the skills, frameworks, and success of that time. The generations that might cultivate a new kind of church are probably not even born yet. Those who must lead in our time are reading this book. How will we respond to this challenge?

THE EXPERIENCE OF TRANSITION

I was sorting through a pile of old papers after my mother died recently and came across a letter about her twenty-year-old brother. The letterhead read *The King's Regiment* and briefly described how he was killed in France at the Battle of Estaires in the valley of the River Lys

---

[24] Mary Jo Leddy, *Reweaving the Religious Life* (Mystic, CT: Twenty-Third Publications, 1990), 3. [Insert added.]

on April 9, 1918. In an obtuse, bureaucratic manner, the letter stated that no body was found for Corporal Robert Crosbie, #200913, DCM, but that his name was engraved on the Loos Memorial in France. My grandmother was unable to adjust to that loss of her young son; she lost her grip on reality for the rest of her life.

Western culture unraveled after World War I. No one was prepared for the new realities an industrialized, technological world would bring to battle. Millions died because generals waged war using plans and scenarios learned from earlier wars when there were no machine guns, mustard gas, tanks, or aircraft. They were so deeply embedded in an older world of gentleman soldiering that they could neither grasp, nor adjust, to the enormity of the changes technology and industrialization were bringing.[25]

Similarly, we cannot address our situation merely by adopting habits, techniques, skills, and experiences from the way the church world functioned in the twentieth century. Something else is needed! Change strategies borrowed from a world of stability misdirect in the world of discontinuous change. Why is this so? What is happening to people living in this transition? What are the dynamics driving people in the midst of such change? What are the skills needed to cultivate a new imagination among God's people in this phase of change? Addressing these questions will open up the frameworks needed to lead God's people in this period.

When people experience discontinuous change they respond by moving in one of two directions to recover their sense of control and stability. They will either:

1) attempt to return or recreate the organization's prior traditions, habits, and way of life, or

2) abandon the old and create a new future to quickly escape the confusion of this in-between phase.

---

[25] See Barbara Tuchman, *The Guns of August* (Toronto: Ballantine, 1994).

The following diagram illustrates each of these directions:

In each case the basic drive is to control the anxiety and ambiguity of transition by escaping it as quickly as possible. Both responses are understandable, but fail to address the unavoidable realities of transition. Both misdirect in terms of discerning how to form communities of God's people in transition. Only by remaining in the midst of the discontinuities and not trying to fix or find answers is it possible to form such communities. Yet this is exactly what both movements want to resist and overcome.

Both groups are present in every congregation along with slight variations upon and/or combinations of the two. Some people demand that the church become like the one down the road that seems to be successful by being more "traditional" or "contemporary" (take your pick); others want to change everything into some radically emergent, next-type-of-church community. Leading in the transition phase, however, is about staying in the center of the discontinuity and understanding what is happening to people in the midst of transition. How do we this?

UNDERSTAND THE ASSUMED FRAMEWORKS SHAPING CONGREGATIONAL LIFE

A formative conviction and practice continues to shape both Liminal and Emergent thinking about change. While we believe that most circumstances of people and their interrelationships are neither linear nor predictable, leaders often still function as if organizations, like congregations, can be managed and controlled by linear, strategic planning processes. Our training and modeling reflexively direct us to respond to discontinuous change with the ingrained patterns and assumptions illustrated in the following diagram:

The instinctive assumption is: when confronted with a problem, it can be solved with a process like the one in the diagram above. The goal of this process is to design a plan to fix the problem based upon a predetermined, preferable future. This is achieved through the following steps:

1) Gather all the information and data possible about the problem.

2) Analyze each element by breaking it down into manageable parts.

3) Develop scenarios based upon the preferred future.

4) Work out a strategic plan to achieve that future.

5) Align all resources, including people and programs, to work the plan.

When we are planning a vacation, constructing a building, designing a program, organizing a sermon series, or planning a field trip to another country, this is a good way to proceed. But when facing discontinuous change, it fails to address what is happening and, therefore, fails to innovate the emergent actions required. It is a process that assumes we are still in a stable environment that allows for rational control and prediction. It is based on the belief that we can, as we did for most of the twentieth century, define, determine, and design the preferred future we want and then align all the elements of our world—congregations, resources, money, people—to get where we want to go.

The problem is that it leaves leadership imagination unaltered. The environment is still treated as if it were a static, manageable plain rather than the turbulent, unchartable waters it is. A turbulent environment is not a *knowable* environment—we lose control and predictability in the midst of discontinuity and transition. This is why we use the language of *emergent*. It describes where we are relative to a future that is in flux. This future is not predictable; it can only be discovered along the way. Therefore, leaders who want to cultivate missional communities in transition must set aside goal-setting and strategic planning as their primary model. Leadership in this context is not about *forecasting*, but about the *formation* of networks of discourse among people. It's about the capacity to engage the realities of people's lives and contexts in dialogue with Scripture. It is about building new connections. The Spirit of God will be in the midst of such dialogues, forming new patterns of communication, relationship, and action as God's people. But it can't be predicted and controlled from this side; the future emerges as people live *in* the ambiguities of transition.

The shift in frameworks, skills, capacities, and habits required of leaders isn't easy, nor will the road be smooth. People are complicated and organizations are complex. People's emotional, inner, nonrational responses play a large role in the transition process. One can't apply change strategies like programs or templates laid over a congregation. Leadership in transition requires adaptive skills that innovate participative dialogue. Such leadership understands change as primarily an emerging process rather than carefully planned movements towards a predefined, preferable future. Emergence cannot be imposed from above; it is cultivated through participation. Leaders must let go of the belief that more information, or more data, or some new program can reestablish control and result in a desired future. It's a new world requiring new skills and capabilities.

UNDERSTAND THE SOURCES OF RESISTANCE TO CHANGE

> When change is driven from above and moves along a predetermined path, or when members of living systems are marched lock-step in frontal assaults on the fortress of adaptive change, these efforts will most likely fail. But a wellgrounded design for emergence provides a very different experience. When properly mobilized, the so called "resistant masses" . . . simply cease to exist as such.[26]

Most people don't want to stay in the transition phase. They will, therefore, look for a leader who promises either a return to the habits and traditions of the immediate past or a different future. In both cases, people are looking for stability, control, and success within their culture. This makes transition challenging. Congregations become places of deep resistance as well as immense hope. In order to engage the hope we must understand the sources of resistance and how they can be addressed.

Look again at the illustration from page 44 showing the difference between *change* and *transition*.

CHANGE *is what happens to us from the outside and over which we usually have no control.*

TRANSITION *is our inner response to the changes we are experiencing and over which we do have some control.*

[26] Pascale et al., *Surfing the Edge of Chaos*, 201.

Again, *change happens to us*. We have little control over it—it's out there, all around us, happening all the time. *Transition* is about our *inner responses* to change. To understand this difference, we must look at two seemingly paradoxical movements that need to occur in congregations simultaneously.

On one side, people must *let go* of habits, values, and patterns of action learned from the past—that known world that has given them identity and stability. This is a very difficult demand that many congregations and denominational systems now face. Until people enter this letting-go process, it will be impossible to move on—they will remain stuck, attempting to recreate past experiences.

On the other side, they also need to *reenter* the primary narratives and traditions of Christian life. These then get us into dialogue with one another and Scripture over what God is intending through all we are experiencing. It is this that gives us the sense of what God's mission is for our place and time and what we are to do about it.

The two are connected. We enter the process of letting go by reentering core stories. The diagram below indicates this interactive dynamic. Note the arrows on each side pulling the system to either *go back to the world it has just lost* or *make a new future*. The key is in keeping in the loop of letting go and reentering the primary narratives.

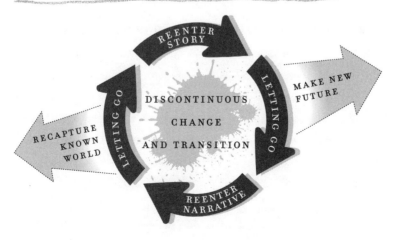

The longer a group has been embedded in a stable relationship with its environment, such as the long Christendom period in North America, the more it gets reshaped into the core stories, values, and habits of that environment. The environment absorbs the group's narratives into its own. Letting go involves understanding how and where this is at work.

In transition, a world comes unglued. Individuals or communities feel disconnected and uprooted from ways of life they love. These changes keep us off-balance, underscoring the experience of being out of control. Assumed values, once taken for granted, are called into question as they no longer seem to work in the transitional world. Accepted moorings become broken havens.

The return to ancient liturgies and worship express this double-edged struggle to reconnect with a tradition. Anchor points that gave Liminals stability become little more than quaint stories to Emergents. While many long for foundations and relationships that are permanent, there is little hope that these can be found. Many Emergents lose the conviction that foundational relationships, like marriage, can last. Those working with youth report an upsurge in the belief that sexuality is no longer a fixed reality of the personality—one has to experiment in order to make up one's sexual style and preference. The direction signs seem to have lost their meaning and the old world has come unglued.

LEADERSHIP IN TRANSITION

Transition can be a place of hope and transformation for us just as the desert wanderings or the Babylonian captivity became places of hope and transformation for Israel. Transition is about our responses to change, rather than simply the change itself. Unfortunately, most leaders want to create change strategies that do not address the core issues of transition. There are important elements of leadership in this place that need to be understood. Leaders must develop the ability to:

    1) Focus on the transition (internal), not just the change (external), by learning to understand how people are responding to

discontinuous change. Liminals and Emergents will have different perspectives on change, but each struggles with the same issues of transition.

2) Connect people's experiences of loss and change with the core stories and traditions of biblical narratives. The interconnection creates an environment in which people can imagine ways of being God's faithful people.

3) Cultivate environments of conversation within which (1) and (2) can occur.

Change creates transition! Habits, patterns, and commitments that have shaped life are hard to let go of. Like the death of a loved one, it is very emotional.

Some years ago my wife and I moved to the West Coast of Canada from Toronto. In so doing, we left our son and daughter in universities back in the East. Whenever my travel schedule allowed it, I would stop in to see them. Every time I had to leave again, I felt a sense of loss more painful than I imagined possible. Often I would watch them walk away as I left and I could hardly believe I'd chosen to move so far away. I wished I could turn the clock back and return to those cozy times at home with my children. Transition is hard!

What confronts the church and its leaders are not just one or two changes; it's a whole world of change all at once. This is our exile *and* our desert. What is this world like for the people in our congregations and those of us who are called to lead among them? To answer this question we turn to the work of anthropologists and their observations of these same processes among pre-modern cultures.

RITES OF PASSAGE IN PRE-MODERN SOCIETIES

When studying pre-modern societies, anthropologist Victor Turner observed their rites of passage rituals.[27] Referring to them as *transition* experiences, he identified three phases:

---

[27] Victor Turner, *The Ritual Process* (Chicago: Aldine Publishing Company, 1974), 94.

1) *Separation*—losing an old-world.

2) *Margin (Liminality)*—entering an unknown world.

3) *Reaggregation*—reemerging into a new world.

Our discussion focuses on the first two. Rites of passage are critical social events in these cultures. Modern societies have lost most rituals for transitioning people from one stage of life to another.

Rites of passage locate us in larger frameworks of meaning—baptism, marriage, and funerals. In pre-modern societies, rites of passage lay at the center of their identity and were filled with religious significance. One important example of such rites of passage was the coming of age rituals for pubescent boys. This illustration provides important insights into our discussion of what happens to people in the midst of discontinuous change.

I. SEPARATION

In pre-modern societies, boys are raised by the females from birth until puberty, with little connection with the adult males. The childhood is shaped by relationships with women who provide a nurturing environment characterized by security and stability. At the onset of puberty, adult males ritually descend on the village and literally snatch the boys from their female world, taking them into isolation deep in the forest. Here the boys have no skills or frameworks to know how to live and survive, yet they must stay there for weeks on their own.

This event signals the end of a stable world. The boys are immediately propelled into an alien world over which they have no control. Their former habits of living no longer work. They are *separated* from the only world they have known and compelled to enter a traumatic, in-between world of transition.

II. LIMINALITY

The next stage is given the technical term: *liminality*. It describes what happens to people *separated* from their known worlds. Liminality was the experience of Robinson Crusoe when he was shipwrecked on a desert island. The shipwreck was his separation from a world he had known and was skilled in managing. The desert island was his liminal state—a place so different that the old rules of living wouldn't help him survive. Even the most experienced sailor, capable of navigating around the world through terrible storms, was now thoroughly disoriented. Liminality is comprised of two elements:

a) **The external event**: An external event/change happens *to* an individual or group. It suddenly thrusts the group to the margins, outside of all its familiar frameworks toward the edge of chaos. Crusoe was shipwrecked, his boat destroyed. His boat symbolizes a stable world that gives meaning, control, and predictability. This external force of discontinuous change disrupts all of life.

b) **Our inner responses to the situation**: Crusoe's initial response was simple bewilderment. For many pastors whose habits, rituals, and ordered life are gone, there can be confusion, bewilderment, depression, and a feeling that one's whole identity has been stolen. How could this have happened?

LIMINALITY: A THRESHOLD EXPERIENCE

Both the event and the inner responses comprise the experience of *liminality*. An individual or group is brought into a new situation: a threshold experience. This is about being placed on the edge of chaos where there is loss and hope, pain and potential. It is a threshold experience because it creates a complex tension between the two poles of wanting to recover the lost past and discover an alternative present.

In the early stages of liminality, the greatest desire of leaders is to recover what has been lost. When a group of people is unwillingly taken from its normal roles and relationships and placed in a location where few of their skills or coping-mechanisms work, they will exhibit some or all of the following responses:

» *Confusion*: A simple experiment helps us understand what happens inside people struggling with liminality. Have them write two sentences quickly dictated to them. Then, have them place the pen in their other hand. Dictate two new sentences quickly, but don't repeat anything. Ask people to describe their experiences. They will report being confused trying to write with the *wrong* hand. Then tell them they must write with this hand for the rest of their lives. This will lead to the next set of responses.

» *Discomfort and anger:* When left in an unknown context where the skills they have learned no longer work, people will typically respond in anger. That anger will be diffused; people will not have had the time or emotional space to understand what is occurring to them. Consequently, they will strike out at whatever, or whoever, symbolizes the source of their discomfort.

» *Instinctive desire to recapture the old world:* Like Dorothy in the *Wizard of Oz*, the Hebrew slaves in the desert outside Egypt, or Crusoe trying to build a boat from the remains of the ruined ship, people want to find a way back home.

Liminality is a place where many of the skills that made our previous life work successfully no longer function. This undermines one's sense of identity because we receive our sense of self from performing well in certain tasks and roles. We are rewarded with position, prestige, money, and identity on the basis of our performance. But in liminality we do not yet know what the new skills and roles will be. We feel like our lives are out of control and threatened—we are no longer sure of who we are or what we are supposed to be doing.

In summary, here is a list of some of the important characteristics of the liminal phase:

1) People always experience it as loss.

2) You cannot rush people through transition. It is a place where people have to live for a time. You must accept that the season must run its course before you will enter the next.

3) The majority of people have no idea what they are experiencing.

4) It is an emotional state. The confusion, disequilibrium, and inner impulse to recapture what has been lost cannot be switched off by information or images of an exciting new world.

5) Leaders too often make the mistake of assuming that strategic plans or more information is all that is required to move on to the next change phase. This is a serious mistake.

6) It is a time of either regression or opportunity, depending on how it is addressed.

DIMINISHED RITUALS—INCREASED CHOICES

It is these inner responses that make the liminal situation so hard. What enables people to move through this transition are the cultural resources lost to modern cultures—it is a larger narrative or religious framework that gives meaning to people in the midst of massive transitions. The global discontinuities and anxieties we face require a larger framework of meaning. In modern societies, the rites of passage and rituals that give people a larger framework of meaning, like marriage, are being displaced or become opaque and confusing. We now live off fragments, reminders of a way of life that has passed. Modernity de-privileges tradition in order to liberate humanity from the perceived "suffocating bonds" that result from what they consider passé rituals and traditions. Once essential for sustaining cultures, rituals and traditions consequently seem little more than echoes of a past. At the moment when pervasive, discontinuous change presses us into liminality, there are fewer and fewer rituals to provide the meaning and frameworks that provide identity.

The church resides within this world and has imbibed much of this ethos. Yet, it is one of the few places in our culture where there remains the possibility of reengaging a larger narrative. It is at this point of possibility that the challenge of our modern world complicates things. Religious frameworks have been split off from the larger public order of life. Religion is privatized and individualized; it is not viewed as a resource for meaning and action outside personal, inner, individual experience. Christianity is no longer communal. Religion has become a consumer product repackaged to meet the needs of the *self*, not to provide a transcendent framework of meaning larger than that self.

The shift from conversation about Christianity to spirituality illustrates this. *Spirituality* is an amorphous word with little content until an individual places his or her own personal meaning in it. It is a shifting symbol made and remade to continually fit the moving need of one's inner self. It is a self-referential, solipsistic shopping basket for the spiritual consumer in the mall of religion.

Consequently, Christian life is increasingly unable to address the crisis of liminality. It has become a profoundly dubious consumer item. The new *seekers* of spiritual products come to religious institutions, like churches, in order to make their lives work with quick strategies to find purpose. They want consumer sound bites that will stop the churning of their worlds. They will resist those who suggest that health requires them to engage the painful process of liminality. Within this individualized, privatized, consumer religious framework, liminality is a series of disruptive events that undermine one's personal, inner spiritual life.

However, as is often the nature with truth, it will take the honesty of facing liminality regardless of the discomfort it causes to embrace the freedom and opportunities it presents. And, despite the increasing individualistic world we live in, we must realize that we cannot do it alone. This is why I believe that the answer doesn't lie in better programs or strategic planning, but instead lies in coming together around Scripture in the last potential phase of liminality—*communitas*.

Reflection and Application

1. Do you have any stories of liminality that you have experienced, had friends who experienced, or seen in the media lately? How did you (they) deal with it? How would you address a similar situation knowing what you do now?

2. How do such times of liminality shatter our frameworks? How did it change the frameworks of the people in the stories from question one? Which adjustments seemed to work best?

3. Why is it that strategic planning comes up short of achieving its goals in times of transition? Give examples where this has happened.

4. Look again at the diagram on page 89. How could you start engaging in this process with your congregation? What biblical narratives might you start with? How do you see engaging in this type of a solution to transition as opposed to a strategic planning approach?

5. Review again what Victor Turner discusses about rights of passage (pages 93 thru 95. How do you see rites of passage such as this as important, even though our culture is largely devoid of them today? Discuss examples of rites of passage from other cultures (example: Jewish bar mitzvah/bat mitzvah). How do such rites bind a community together and address our times of transition?

CHAPTER

7

LIMINALITY AND
COMMUNITAS

A 45-year-old senior vice president for development in a church-based organization returns from a trip to be informed by the president that her services are no longer required. An envelope is passed across the desk with information about an agency that can help her deal with transition; negotiations begin for severance pay. At forty-five, she has entered liminality.

You're a senior in college, completing an honors degree in art history. You're reading postmodern theorists like Derrida, Foucault, and Bourdieu. You have grown up in a church. Your parents are now divorced and the church back home is fighting over music, forms of baptism, and who can be a member. How can you form a meaning system amidst these competing, confusing values? What might it look like?

Michael has been the pastor of a small rural church in eastern Pennsylvania for two years. He's instituted some changes in the worship styles, office staff, and the forms of meetings. But now the small community is being inundated by radically different kinds of people. They are urban professionals moving out to find cheaper housing. They have huge commutes every day into the city, and their lives move to a radical-ly different tune from the rest of the congregation members. Michael now finds that while his previous skills as a pastor worked well for the small, aging congregation, neither experience nor his training equipped him to connect all these new dots. What can he do in the midst of competing demands, needs, expectations, and models of being the church?

Across our society, both church systems and the people within them are struggling with transition and liminality in their lives. Everyone in congregational and denominational leadership is aware of the depth of anxiety, confusion, and anger that now pervades people's lives.

One denominational executive, when asked what issues present the most difficulty for him in bringing about change, said:

> It's the whole culture in which we serve. There is so much change that people are overwhelmed with what is happening. Our people, from good, old European backgrounds, now find themselves almost living in a different country in the very neighborhoods they've been in all their lives. It's very hard for people to fig-ure out what to do. ... We are not well-traveled in this world and keep doing the same things over and over again even when we know they don't work.

People feel increasingly vulnerable in their everyday lives; their relational networks are growing frail and they feel increasingly unable to deal with new forces over which they seem to have no control.

This liminal context will be with us for a long time to come. The normative structures of congregational and denominational life have been breaking down for some time. Like Israel in its Exodus experience, this process takes time. It took many years for Israel to reach a point in Egypt where they realized that their position was no longer tenable. While the actual shift from Egypt to the desert was quite brief and filled with exaltation, the real work began in the desert. The transition from one state to another (from Egypt to the Promised Land) took more than a generation.

Both Liminals and Emergents are in the same transition even though each have different experiences of what that means. How do we lead denominational systems and congregations in this place? A part of the answer lies in another feature of liminality: *communitas*.

LIMINALITY AND COMMUNITAS

Turner's studies of the rites of passage in pre-modern cultures describe the stages pubescent boys move through when forcibly set in a liminal context. The description offers important clues about how Liminals and Emergents might engage one another. The term *communitas* describes a latter, potential phase of liminality. *Communitas* is about what can happen to the relationships among a divergent group undergoing discontinuous change together. They can experience a deeper connection of community. Here are some basic principles of how people function in groups and organizations striving towards *communitas*.

THE DIALECTIC PROCESS BETWEEN STRUCTURE AND *COMMUNITAS*

All groups—whether a sports team, a denominational staff, a work group at the office, or the staff at a hospital—eventually differentiate into roles within an organization. These roles, over time, take on clear functions. For example, the word *pastor* conjures up a set of skills, abilities, and expectations that have been the standard for leading our churches during the last few centuries. The role of pastor has to do with preaching, teaching, caring, nurturing, visiting shut-ins and the sick, and counseling, along with the ability to marry and bury people. This role may have more or fewer requirements and nuances in different settings, but generally this framework would describe it in most modern societies.

Over time, roles become differentiated into habitual performance expectations so that members of the culture and its organizations can carry on their important work without reinventing themselves every time they turn around. Consequently, in stable societies these roles are developed to a high degree. People are rewarded based on the hierarchy of privilege and leadership. A classic illustration of this process is the relationship between the master and the apprentice. While we tend not to use this language anymore in our egalitarian societies, it expresses the embedding of roles within hierarchies of value and importance. Societies tend to establish stable, repeatable performance roles to make the society work with high levels of efficiency.

The table below illustrates how this works. It is a simple diagram of how the church functioned as a corporate organization in the long period of social stability within North America across most of the twentieth century.

Organizations are formed out of the cultural environment. Thus, the organizational structures of the Middle Ages were very different from those of the twentieth century. The model can be summarized as follows:

> 1) Different cultures have different sets of values and
> expectations that shape their imaginations.

2) Organizations (like congregations and denominations) are developed to serve the requirements of a culture at a specific time.

3) Leadership roles are developed so that the organization performs with a high level of efficiency in delivering the desired values and goods to the culture.

The cultural environment determines the specific shape an organization will take. This, in turn, determines the roles people have in that organization. In long periods of stability, organizational forms and roles are embedded in the habits and values of the culture, and come to be seen as the universal and standard ways things have been and should always be. The culture then rewards those organizations and those roles that perform with excellence and give the culture what it wants.

The organizational culture of the twentieth century is summarized in the following table:

ENVIRONMENT	» STABLE » PREDICTABLE » DEVELOPMENTAL
ORGANIZATIONAL CULTURE	» HIERARCHIES » BUREAUCRACIES » MANAGERS / EXPERTS » TOP-DOWN FLOW » ALIGN THROUGH STRATEGIC PLANNING » LINEAR
LEADERSHIP FUNCTIONS	» MANAGE PEOPLE » OPTIMIZE PERFORMANCE » CONTROL STRUCTURE

For most of the twentieth century, North America, protected by two oceans, as well as being the economic and technological center of the world, functioned within a stable, managed, controlled, and relatively predictable environment. Within this environment, the cultural assumption was that the North American genius was its ability to create a world that could give its citizens the good things in life. This was accomplished through the corporation, developed as a new organizational structure near the beginning of the twentieth century.

Since the early part of the twentieth century, most church bodies adapted themselves around this model of organizational life (with basically the same goal—to efficiently provide their members with spiritual goods and services through a centralized structure managed by experts and professionals). This corporate form became the deeply embedded imagination of the culture. For most of the twentieth century, it performed brilliantly giving the American people the good things in life. Leadership roles and functions developed to fit the needs of this corporate organization. Most pastors and church executives learned these roles and took them as the standard way in which to run an effective church system. The church rewarded leaders who exhibited high levels of ability in these functions.

The world that made this cultural stability and organizational form possible rapidly lost its legitimacy by the early 1980s. It disappeared with incredible speed in the final decades of the twentieth century. This transition was understood within sectors of the culture—such as the business world—but the churches failed to grasp how deeply they had been shaped by this culture and that it had lost its legitimacy. The end of that world thrust us into a liminal situation. The diagram below suggests some of the contours of these transformations and illustrates the massive changes required in both organization form and the roles people have within the context.

	FUNCTIONAL 20TH CENTURY CHURCH TECHNICAL SKILLS	EMERGING MISSIONAL CHURCH ADAPTIVE SKILLS
ENVIRONMENT	»STABLE »PREDICTABLE »DEVELOPMENTAL	»UNSTABLE »DISCONTINUOUS »EMERGENT
ORGANIZATIONAL CULTURE	»HIERARCHIES »BUREAUCRACIES »MANAGERS / EXPERTS »TOP-DOWN FLOW »ALIGN THROUGH STRATEGIC PLANNING »LINEAR	»NETWORKS »TEAMS »DIALOGUE/CONSCIOUS LEARNING »BOTTOM-UP FLOW »CULTIVATED VARIETY »NON-LINEAR DYNAMICS
LEADERSHIP FUNCTIONS	»MANAGE PEOPLE »OPTIMIZE PERFORMANCE »CONTROL STRUCTURE	»MANAGE PEOPLE »OPTIMIZE PERFORMANCE »CONTROL STRUCTURE

THE FIVE STAGES OF LIMINALITY

This brings us back to Turner's observations of what takes place within liminality. There are distinct stages.

First, a group or culture is thrust from its stable world into a place where they've never been before and for which they have few, if any, preparations. The shift of organizational life in modern societies late in the last century was one of those transitions. Confusion and anxiety are the primary responses; a group tries to get back to its stable world or escape into some devised future.

Second, hierarchies and roles effective in the prior context crumble, neither functioning as they did nor providing the status positions normal to the former system. The role identities that gave people position, privilege, authority, and power no longer provide positional legitimacy or guarantee the outcomes they once did. Prior forms of relational and organizational hierarchies cease to function, even though people keep trying to make them work. One pastor of a denomination that, only a short time ago, was labeled one of the fastest growing in the U.S., put it this way: "We once thought of ourselves as the fastest growing church in America; now we feel dead in the water. The wine has run out. Things are not as they were."

Third, this precipitates a crisis within the systems and groups. This crisis can be viewed in a number of different ways. The diagram below illustrates what is happening to the organization overall.

The American church has been shifted from the center of stability and equilibrium in our culture out toward the edge where its overall experience is now chaotic. The reason for the chaos is that the norms that had previously given identity, power, authority, and position don't function outside the equilibrium. The former professional positioning of people in a hierarchy is now called into question.

This is what many of the Emergents are doing to Liminal leaders and their organizational systems. The Liminals are often threatened by this challenging of their authority and position by younger, "inexperienced" leaders. The temptation is to resist or default to authority or find ways of putting the Emergents on the outside.

On the other side, Emergents tend to miss the dynamic taking place; they tend to define themselves by being "over-against." The technical term is *anti-structure*. This doesn't mean Emergents don't have any structure, but that they act and create practices that go against the existing forms and structures. Thus, many Emergents, coming from evangelical backgrounds, seek ancient forms of liturgy as a means of connecting with a different life structure from that in which they were raised.

The anti-structure process is one way in which those who feel the push toward the edge confront those who continue to hold onto former positions, forms, and practices. Unfortunately, few in either tribe understand or manage what is happening, so the tendency for the two groups is to diverge, objectifying and blaming the other side for the shortcomings and failures of the church to be relevant to today's culture.

Fourth, at this point in the liminal stage, there is a dialectical tension between two sides. On the one side is the experience of liminality: the loss of structure, organization, and identity. On the other side is the pull towards structure where control, order, stability, and hierarchy reside. The following diagram illustrates what is happening:

```
LIMINALITY  &  STRUCTURE
A  DIALECTICAL  PROCESS
```

LIMINALITY ⟷ STRUCTURE

» UNDIFFERENTIATED

» LACK OF FORM/ORDER

» LOSS OF POSITION/ROLE

» DIFFERENTIATED

» HIERARCHY/ORDER

» POSITION/ROLE

This is a continuum which is dialectical, that is, each side interacts with and affects the other. In fact, the one will create the other. A system that has stayed in stability and structure for a long time will, eventually, create a counter action towards the liminality. This is part of the anti-structure of the Emergents. Emergents move from informal gatherings based around relationships and undifferentiated engagements toward asking questions of how they can give more form and structure to what they are doing.

Some Emergents fear this process and fight for the continuation of anti-structure and undifferentiated engagements that remain as open-ended as possible. The tension here is that a few highly-gifted and skilled people among the Emergents can maintain this open-ended ambiguity, but the vast majority of Emergents who have been attracted into this environment and these values have no idea what to do. They become desperate for some form of structure and formation in order to move forward. Without this they enter into experiments that are ill-conceived and potentially hurtful for themselves and those involved.

Liminals, on the other hand, continue trying to return themselves and their systems back to the center of stability and equilibrium. They want to diminish the experience of chaos, but in so doing miss the fact that this experience of chaos is probably the only place from which imagination, creativity, and innovation can emerge. The Liminals tend to look for models that others have developed and then apply these in their own setting. The hope and expectation is that this move will fix the chaos and reinstitute success.

Liminality is not a permanent condition. It lasts for a period, then things shift back to some form of structure and hierarchy. This is a necessary, constructive process. When the window of liminality is open, it is a potential *threshold* within which the imagination and creativity of God's people might call forth something genuinely new. A threshold is a moment, or space, in which, for a time, the old forms and critiques can be put aside for something genuinely new to emerge. But each side of the dialectic needs the other. In fact, they are intimately interconnected. The key here is for both Liminals and Emergents to understand what is actually happening and to dialogue about it. This leads to the next stage of liminality.

Fifth, if members of these two groups can comprehend what is happening—namely, that each group, in different ways, is jointly undergoing transition and liminality—then the doors open to the potential of dialogue. This dialogue in the midst of the liminal situation can call forth what Turner calls *communitas*: the potential for people to discover one another on a very different level of identity and role than from the previous period.

Communitas is the potential and threshold for Emergents and Liminals at this moment in North America. It is a new kind of *commons*, an *open space* where we might discover and learn from one another in powerfully innovative ways. The idea of a *commons* is an ancient one that is being rediscovered. The *commons* is an archaic, unfamiliar idea for most of us. But this strangeness is appropriate—it helps us all find a neutral vocabulary over the language we each use to identify our particular tribe. We currently lack a hopeful vocabulary that doesn't get in the way of talking with one another.

The *commons* refers to those spaces (land, ideas, values, relationships) open to ordinary people—they are *collectively* owned. What happened in the early industrial age in Europe is that the commons got *enclosed:* privatized, traded in the market, turned into a commodity for the use of one group as opposed to another (for example: the Emergents *own* the postmodern or the new; the Liminals *own* the structures or the old). It is about the exclusive appropriation by one group of previously collective-ly-owned experiences, imagination, and resources.

Today there is a rediscovery of the idea of the commons as a way of dialoging about issues that are important for all of us. Surely we can do this as Liminals and Emergents bound together as God's people in a strange new world. This new commons is a place, therefore, of both opportunity and danger. Here are some of the issues that might be present in these commons:

OPPORTUNITY	DANGER
Move out of established positions.	*React defensively; defend established positions.*
Embrace the ambiguity and chaos of heterogeneity in terms of varying ideas and understanding without needing to be defensive of one's own place and position.	*Opt to create a new homogeneity within one's systems and organizations in terms of unspoken values and expectations.*
Let go of position and status (both Emergents and Liminals have these in their own ways).	*Emphasize and live out of position and status.*
Work together outside the normal boundaries and expectations of habitual structures with groups of people from different levels and walks of life. »Form loose coalitions drawn together by pursuit of elusive dream that seems out of reach. »Develop high levels of social interaction across difference. »Be ad hoc. »All are generalists. »An absence of hierarchies. »Learn how to excel together in ambiguous environments with multiple challenges. »Let strategy emerge.	*Emphasize status; move into silos.* *Focus on an "us-them" polarity.* *Major on clichés:* »Modern postmodern »Conservative revolutionary »Institutional emergent *Focus on the following:* »Structure as a corporate organization »Large-scale, strategic (not "just-in-time") planning »Specialization of roles and programs »Ability to perform »Organizational hierarchies not loose teams »Experts »Lower levels of social interaction »Rationalized planning

There are few who don't recognize that the coalitions, structures, and forms of church life need to be reimagined. The potential of *communitas* is for something innovative to emerge across the differences that have characterized the last several decades of church life in North America. *Communitas* is the willingness of people to risk entering a new commons where they journey together as God's pilgrim people in order to discern together the future that God's Spirit might be bringing forward to them. It calls for a willingness from leaders on both sides of the polarity to recognize the gifts of the other and a readiness to submit themselves as novices to each other. This is uncommon at the moment; however, it is possible.

When Moses encountered God in the burning bush, his entire world of safety, control, and identity shattered. He had accommodated himself to a world that was never meant to be his destiny. He had to face the greatest fear of his life—to return to Egypt—and demand of the powerful empire that God's people be set free. That empire could no longer own the people of God—it was a time for change.

Moses was shaken by God's request. He needed some sign to prove he had authority and power, but he also wanted some control over the encounter with the empire. So Moses asked for God's name. In that culture, to have a person's name was to have their authority. Moses was asking for control over God's purposes. God's response was to tell the slaves that *ehyah asher ahyah* had sent him. The normal translation is: *I am who I am*. Another way of translating this enigmatic name is: *I shall be there, as there I shall be*. It is ambiguous language. It can mean: "Moses, it's none of your business what my name is—your business is to go and do as you are told. Let Me take care of who is in control."

There were two sides to this naming of God. One was the covenantal promise of God that even in the most difficult and threatening of places, God's presence could be counted on. The other suggests God will never be present as we anticipate or wish. When obeying God, the future cannot be the future of our own making and control. The way forward will never be an extension of our needs, positions, or roles. The future is God's future and so God will be there as God will be there. *Communitas* is where leaders no longer hold onto their roles, identities, and needs to control, but dare to be formed into a journeying people by *I shall be there as there I shall be.*

REFLECTION AND APPLICATION

1. Describe the concept of *communitas* in your own words. How does it differ from our normal sense of community? Why is it more important?

2. Why do predetermined roles and hierarchies interfere with the cultivation of *communitas?* Why do inflexible systems and structures interfere with the cultivation of *communitas?*

3. Why is imagination and experimentation more likely to succeed coming out of a *communitas* of Liminals and Emergents working together than either group working on their own? What assets do Liminals bring to Emergents in this forum? What assets do the Emergents bring?

4. Why do liminality and structure conflict? Why must structure loosen considerably before *communitas* can take place?

5. Where could you create a commons in your church? In your community? Who else could participate in it? What would be some values of it that would contribute to the creativity and experimentation that comes out of it?

LIMINALITY AND *COMMUNITAS* IN SCRIPTURE

Transition and liminality are not new—they are part of the life of all individuals, groups, and organizations. The continuum between liminality and structure is always present. In fact, it is at work throughout Scripture. God continually engages across this continuum in formatting a people. A danger of liminality is to think our situation is unique, thus isolating ourselves from others who have gone through the exact same thing and could offer help. The church's current place of loss and confusion is not unique, but part of the way God has continually engaged God's people. By entering Scriptures together, it is possible to see how familiar patterns of liminality were at work in the most formative narratives of our faith.

What might we hear and learn of God's purposes if we allow Scripture to speak to us from this perspective? What might happen among a group of God's people if they allow a *communitas* to form around reading Scripture together from the perspective of our present phase of transition?

Earlier, we said there are two, seemingly paradoxical movements that occur in the transition phase of the change cycle before *communitas* can be experienced. On the one side, a group is *separated* from the world (way of life, habits, attitudes, assumptions, practices) it has known and thrived. The early stages of liminality are about people's grief, confusion, anger, and resistance to this loss. The instinctive need is to recover what has been lost in order to return their world to a stable, manageable, and predictable environment. The critical piece is for the group to reach a point where it recognizes that this return is no longer possible.

This, in turn, creates a crisis of awareness: the group knows it cannot return, but neither does it know what to do or how to proceed. The dilemma is that neither people nor leaders can live in this state for very long without needing to do something to either fix or change the situation. This is when congregations, leaders, and even denominational systems quickly turn to programs taken from elsewhere to change the reality of their situation. In other words, they attempt to resolve the crisis by adopting some kind of outside system that is perceived to be a solution. This action not only doesn't provide the answer they are looking for, but also short-circuits the potential of liminality.

Some denominations, confronted with the hemorrhaging of membership and dollars develop BHAGs ("Big Hairy Audacious Goals") such as a plan to plant a thousand new congregations across the U.S. over the next ten years. Unfortunately, this kind of goal setting doesn't fix the crisis. They are attempts to escape liminality and avoid the true interaction that could result in *communitas*.

People whom I have counseled on this often respond, "What *do* we do then? If strategic planning and programs don't work, then what *do* we do? It's fine to critique, but what actions *can* and *should* one take?" These are legitimate questions. Neither leaders nor congregational systems can be left with simply a critique of what they are doing with no direction as to where to go next.

This is where the second part of the paradox becomes critical, because it is about a certain form of action, namely, listening again to the primary narratives of our tradition. For Christian communities this is, first and foremost, through Scripture. In liminality there are other alternatives to those given above. Congregations and the systems that serve them do not have to jump into BHAGs or other such strategies. The alternative involves coming together, in a context of *communitas*, to reenter the primary narratives of Scripture to hear *together* what God may be saying.

This reentering of Scripture is essential if:

a) a genuine form of *communitas* is to emerge in the midst of the church,

b) the temptation of jumping to programmatic strategies is to be avoided, and

c) we are to hear together what the Spirit may be calling forth among us.

To a large extent, leaders are focusing their anxiety and confusion around liminality toward addressing *church* questions—What should the church be? What is the nature of the church? What does it mean to be the people of God? Thus, the questions that most church leaders want their people to bring to Scripture are *church* questions that miss the real issues of liminality affecting most people's lives. This is why church feels irrelevant to most people. Furthermore, Scripture is silenced for most people or it just seems to be an irrelevant set of stories about things that aren't that critical. Leaders who focus on programs and strategies to make the church *work* fail to understand how Scripture is the most powerful source of life formation and imagination in the midst of liminality.

The following sections illustrate how reengaging the narratives of God's actions in Scripture formed alternative futures of the kingdom among God's people. Through these illustration you will see:

» a hopeful way of embedding ourselves back into our primary narratives and providing people with the stability of the story rather than programs;

» why our liminality is not a terrible mistake or the absence of the Spirit, but a sign that God is at work in the church right now;

» a developing picture of how an alternative future can emerge that is rooted in God's people as they engage their own stories with those of the Scriptures; and

» a direction for leadership, namely, the cultivation of an environment in which the Scripture might address us as God's people in the realities of our experience.

ILLUSTRATIONS FROM SCRIPTURE

THE EXODUS

The Exodus story is a paradigm of liminality. It is about God's people in the midst of massive transition.

Israel, from the time of Jacob's move into Egypt under the protection of Joseph to the hardship of slavery hundreds of years later, had formed a particular identity that took generations to develop. By Moses' time, they were both suffering profoundly and thoroughly acculturated to their Egypt situation.

This is the paradox of their situation. It was both deeply painful and, at the same time, the only way of life they knew. The stories of the patriarchs must have been like distant, disconnected memories—not an empowering vision that could direct their lives, but a nostalgic, displaced history that must have seemed like fairy tales. Egypt and slavery were their real story; these were the central features of their identity as a people. As strange as it may seem, their stable, predictable, almost manageable word was Egypt, not the Promised Land. In spite of the suffering, this had been the world of regularity and normality for several generations. There was predictability to the roles and events that took place in the daily scheme of survival within this system—freedom was a totally foreign concept to them.

The escape from Egypt was both release and separation. It was both exhilarating and anxiety-producing. The desert narratives present a confused, frightened assortment of people living in the midst of terrifying fear precisely because Egypt had been taken from them. Even though Egypt represented the very world that was destroying them, they wanted to return to its secure predictability. By contrast, the desert was a terrifying place, without form and without hope. They had no preparation and no skills to live in this strange, terrifying place. As a result, they defaulted to blaming one another for their predicament.

How could any leader have been capable of taking people from the security of their known world to this horrible place where all must die? Forty years of desert wandering would be needed to work through this issue. Only as a generation that had never known Egypt emerged was it possible to come together in forms of *communitas* that might cultivate a different imagination about what God was doing with them. It would be these offspring who entered the Promised Land. What was little more than a month's journey by foot would take forty years. It required that much time for four hundred years of Egypt to be removed from the collective soul of this people.

The desert wanderings have all the characteristics of a people working their way through liminality. Leaving Egypt was experienced as loss, ending, and death, because it was all they had known for generations. How do a people imagine anything else if their founding stories become a faint memory? All along the way, Israel resisted the leadership of Moses, consistently seeking to reverse the direction of their journey. The slavery of a known Egypt was preferred to ambiguity of an old man's promise.

Eventually, however, the desert forged a people for whom transition became the norm. They became adaptive and anticipated an alternative future. Along the way of this liminal journey, Israel became a pilgrimage people. At the mountain they received the Law and were given directions for the form of life that would shape them as God's people. In other words, in the midst of the desert, they were not given a strategic plan but something radically different. They received:

> » a liturgy which provided the frame for God to form them into a different kind of people from those who left Egypt;

> » signs and symbols—the Ark of the Covenant, manna in the desert, the Tabernacle, the fire by night and cloud by day—that formed a constant, present reminder of who they were compared to all the other peoples of the world—in other words, their identity and memory were being formed; and

> » practices they carried out each day, week, and month which resocialized them into being the distinct people of God.

Out of these gifts from God was formed a people, a *communitas*, able to dream of the possibilities that the land of future promise held.

THE PERIOD OF THE JUDGES

In those generations immediately following entry to the land, Israel lived in a loose tribal confederacy linked together through the Covenant and their common worship. When external threat arose, God would call forth a judge who led the people in dealing with it. In one sense, this period was one in which a high level of stability existed between the great empires. For Israel, this was a great gift, for the land lay astride not just the great trade routes, but also the very place nations wanted to control. This environment of stability gradually began to erode, though, as new empires emerged. The loose confederacy found itself squeezed between competing armies, global politics, and a struggle for land.

In this new place, Israel opted out of the political system that had served them for so long. The reason for this change was their incapacity to cope with the threat of seeming chaos and conflict in the midst of fast-changing global political realities. Israel opted for the apparent security of a king who could raise an army, make treaties, and protect the people. In other words, several generations after entering the land, they opted for a security that promised stability and success rather than living in a dependant ambiguity of waiting for God to raise up a judge as God saw fit to meet their needs.

RUTH

The story of Ruth breaks the boundaries of expectation; it is utterly contrary to the way things ought to work in the minds of Israel and her leaders. No one, after entering this story, can believe that God's future emerges from careful strategies crafted within existing frameworks for the purpose of developing a preferable future. But what is clear about this story is that God's future almost always emerges in the most God-forsaken of places. The location of God's purposes, the imagination for God's future, always seems to be present in those people and places that are the most inauspicious and, by all rational calculations, from where nothing of the sort could honestly be expected.

This should be a source of tremendous hope and encouragement for those of us who live in the twilight of a Christendom America convinced that all the great plans and programs for success are moving in the wrong direction. The last places from which we would today expect God to provide answers to us are the congregations across America filled with leaders and people who, in the language of some Emergents, "just don't get it" and "are captives to the American Empire and its values", or, in the language of some Liminals, those "who haven't been trained, don't have experience and don't know what they're doing."

Ruth and her mother-in-law, Naomi, are in a radically liminal situation. They have been separated from everything that gave them security and identity in their world. All the customary had been eradicated from their lives. They are socially, relationally, and economically outside the world they had known. Ruth, whose Hebrew husband had died, is an outsider to Israel with no place in the covenant community. Naomi's solution to this great loss and anxiety was to set Ruth free to return to her former life among the Moabites where she might recover some security in a new marriage. But Ruth, for reasons that are not expressed, elects to bind herself to Naomi instead. Ruth's words express the form of *communitas* we need to discover together as Liminals and Emergents:

> *Then Naomi said to her two daughters-in-law, "Go back, each of you, to your mother's home. May the Lord show kindness to you, as you have shown to your dead and to me. May the Lord grant that each of you will find rest in the home of another husband."*
>
> *Then she kissed them and they wept aloud and said to her, "We will go back with you to your people."*
>
> *But Naomi said, "Return home, my daughters. Why would you come home with me? Am I going to have any more sons, who could become your husbands? Return home, my daughters; I am too old to have another husband." . . .*
>
> *But Ruth replied, "Don't urge me to leave you or turn back from you. Where you go I will go, and where you stay I will stay. Your people will be my people and your God my God. Where you die I will die, and there I will be buried. May the Lord deal with me be it ever so severely, if anything but death separates you and me."*
>
> —*Ruth 1:8-12, 16-17 NIV*

It was from this *communitas* between two women of radically different ages and tribal groups that God's future emerges. When the lineage of Jesus is presented in the gospels, it declares that the concrete, material ways in which God was from the beginning unfolding the mystery behind all creation was among these two women. These nobodies who, in the extremity of their situation, did not resort to Naomi's fix-it plan, but entered into a *communitas* out of which emerged God's future. This is what must happen in North America among Liminals and Emergents.

THE EXILE

As we have already discussed in some detail, another transition experience is that of the exile. In 587 B.C., Nebuchadnezzar laid waste Jerusalem, tearing down its walls and destroying the Temple. The best and brightest from Jerusalem were then taken captive to Babylon. Jeremiah, Isaiah, Daniel, Ezra, and Nehemiah offer a constellation of narratives describing God's dealings with these captives. Jeremiah and Isaiah are accounts of their imposed liminality and how they responded.

What is fascinating about these narratives is how they present the spectrum of possible responses to liminality. There are those who continued to overcome their separation with multiple attempts at returning to Jerusalem to restore the old glory. There are those who quickly bought into the new environment of Babylon, adapted to its world, and created a life that assimilated old beliefs with Babylonian culture. Then there were those who, in the midst of terrible pain and incredible confusion, began to form a *communitas* that reentered their primary narratives, but this time from the perspective of liminality rather than stability and equilibrium.

Separation for these people was sudden, catastrophic, and, seemingly, without warning. The absolutely unthinkable happened in the flash of an eye—Jerusalem was destroyed and Judah taken into exile. This removal, Jeremiah announces, was not the result of geopolitical realities, the armies of powerful kings, or the relentless expansion of empires. It was God's action against God's own people. This reading of the chaos placed the events within a very different framework from what would have been the common interpretation. If this was something more than power politics, then what did it mean for the *covenant* people? If this was God's action, then was *God* abandoning his own people? If that was the case, then here was a catastrophe of unimaginable proportions.

Israel had simply assumed God's presence and protection of both themselves and the land because of who their fathers were. This had been the covenant promise. God was on their side; they were a city on the hill, a light for all the nations. How could anything alter that reality? How could anything go wrong?

Over years, their assimilation and compromise to the cultural assumptions and religious powers of the surrounding peoples had corrupted their understanding of God's purposes. The covenant relationship—expressed in festivals, worship days, and great feasts—had been emptied of their realities and cultural memory. Instead, these festivals, feasts, and rituals had become functions disconnected from the framing stories of the great acts of God's deliverance and promises. By the time of Jeremiah, they were merely external habits that satisfied traditional requirements. Priests and court prophets functioned as regulatory agencies ensuring the structures and rules of the system were maintained appropriately. Right performance displaced covenant faithfulness; ritual replaced meaning.

Though the exile involved only a small percentage of Judah's population, its impact was experienced as a profound assault on the central assumptions of the nation. Their theological frameworks were unable to comprehend what had happened. It was only the poetry and theology of the counter theology of people like Jeremiah who could give meaning to what had happened, even though at first they wanted to ignore them. Nothing in the long period of accommodation prepared the people for exile. This is why Jeremiah's warnings and performances initially fell on deaf ears. His enactments and announcements were beyond the framework Israel had accepted until their point of separation.

Psalm 137 expresses the depth of confusion, anger, and bitterness of a people undergoing separation and liminality. Take a minute to look at the people's heart cry from exile:

> *By the rivers of Babylon—*
> *there we sat down and there we wept*
> *when we remembered Zion.*

On the willows there
we hung up our harps.
For there our captors
asked us for songs,
and our tormentors asked for mirth, saying,
"Sing us one of the songs of Zion!"

How could we sing the LORD'S song
in a foreign land?
If I forget you, O Jerusalem,
let my right hand wither!
Let my tongue cling to the roof of my mouth,
if I do not remember you,
if I do not set Jerusalem
above my highest joy.

Remember, O LORD, against the Edomites
the day of Jerusalem's fall,
how they said, "Tear it down! Tear it down!
Down to its foundations!"
O daughter Babylon, you devastator!
Happy shall they be who pay you back
what you have done to us!
Happy shall they be who take your little ones
and dash them against the rock!

Here were a people utterly at a loss to know how to function. *How do you sing the Lord's song in a strange land?* Their hearts were filled with grief, confusion, and anxiety; their minds were turned toward blame, revenge, and plans to get back to Jerusalem as quickly as possible. There was no sense that they believed for a moment that God's future could be found in the place of exile. In their liminality was the prophet of the margins, Jeremiah, who articulated the shape of hope that would only be found if they entered and embraced the very place where everything seemed to scream of the absence and abandonment of God. The letter to the exiles was from the Lord; it was a call to remain in liminality, for only in that location could there be any possibility of knowing the new place to which God was calling them.

Those who continued longing for the old empire of Jerusalem could not see God's purposes. All the plans to return, all the schemes to jump over and escape the exile were roads that would take these people away from discovering God's purposes in allowing their capture. Only by remaining *in* Babylon would it be possible for them to understand the future of Jerusalem and the purposes of God.

Two critical things happened in Babylon. First, some of the people—the Liminals—began to reenter the primary stories of Israel, but this time from the place of loss and confusion rather than authority and control. Over a period of years, Babylon became the most generative place for the rediscovery and reinterpretation of Scripture for Israel. From this, a new imagination would emerge. Second, there was born in Babylon a generation that was not a part of the glory days of Jerusalem. These became the people, through the generative work of reentering Scripture, who began to imagine a different future for Jerusalem. Here again, both Liminals and Emergents came together in *communitas,* and out of that interrelationship God's alternative future emerged.

In this Babylonian *communitas*, the stories of God's dealings with Israel and the memory of the people was recovered and filtered through the Babylonian experience. What emerged was a radically different reading of the original stories. A new vision of the future emerged in which all creation and all of history were shaped around the triumph of God's kingdom through a covenant people. These were a newly-invented people shaped by a newly discovered Scripture. These people were compelled to rethink and reimagine the meaning of their original primary stories in the light of their world. They recovered tradition, not from the perspective of empire and Jerusalem, but from the liminal identity of exile. This is what made them radical—the reality of their location outside ascendancy and empire where it was no longer possible to fix the past or create some new future. From the margins, after seventy years of painful theological work, came the reformation of Israel as a new, powerful, and more transcendent spiritual nation.

PETER

Peter, prior to the resurrection, lived within frameworks that pre-determined what he heard from and how he responded to Jesus. So embedded was this picture in Peter's mind that he was prepared to set Jesus straight in his thinking and legislate by the sword the nature of the kingdom that Jesus preached was coming. Following the resurrection, Peter's world was turned upside down. This was clearly the case in Acts, where questions about the relationship between Judaism and the Gospel of Jesus, and between Jews and Gentiles, were being worked out. By the time Luke had finished this narrative, Jewish Christianity was a spent force and receding memory. How had the good news of Jesus, a Jew who came from God as the fulfillment of the Jewish Scriptures, become dis-embedded so quickly from its origins? This needed explanation, espe-cially for a Gentile Christian audience confused by this unexpected turn of events.

Luke writes his two-volume account—the book of Luke and the Acts of the Apostles—in part, to address these questions. In Acts 10, Peter is summoned to Joppa where a disciple named Tabitha (Dorcas), loved for the ways she did good and looked after the poor, had died. The expecta-tion was that Peter had authority to raise her from the dead. This is, in fact, what took place, resulting the conversion of many in that city.

Peter was continuously involved in a vital, dynamic movement of God's Spirit that must have been shifting many of his assumptions about the nature and purpose of Jesus' resurrection. All of this must have caused a tremendous stir in the Jewish communities, confirming for many the rightness of their identity and the blessing of God on their lives. But all this initial activity took place solely within the parameters of Judaism. Acts 11:19 makes this clear. Those scattered following Stephen's stoning were limited to proclaiming the Gospel to Jews only. The Gospel remained embedded within the frameworks of Judaism and the understanding of a religious-political renewal of Israel centered in a revitalized Jerusalem.

In Acts 10, however, Peter is separated from this framework. The energy, celebration, and joy of experiencing all that God had promised coming to fruition within the framework of his expectations was shattered. While he was fasting and praying on a rooftop in Joppa, Peter has a vision of the large sheet filled with clean and unclean animals that the Lord tells him to eat. This pushed Peter outside the boundaries and categories of his known world. One of Luke's purposes in recounting this story is to show troubled Gentile Christians that the Gospel had forever broken the boundaries between Jews and Gentiles. It crossed traditional frameworks, turning worlds inside out. How else could the rejection of Judaism and the eventual destruction of Jerusalem be explained?

Peter's vision on the rooftop is about the way in which God's Spirit confronts a religiously-constructed world whose practices have become obstacles to the mission of the kingdom. Jewish Christians, like Peter, were deeply embedded in the stability and normalcy of their constructed world. Peter was confronted with his own boundaries. Standing before Cornelius and watching the Spirit of God falling upon the Gentiles, his inherited framework of coming to God shattered. The Spirit broke down the defining walls of his world. Cornelius manifested the Spirit in ways that had been seen only among Jewish converts. A Gentile was accepted into Christian identity without the need for circumcision. Peter could not have missed the meaning of the Spirit's descent upon those in Cornelius' household. It was a second Pentecost.

This story was also about the conversion of Peter the Christian with an ethnic view of the Gospel, into Peter the Christian shaped by a Gospel greater than the boundaries of his ethnicity or blood. All Peter could do was acknowledge the facts and humbly receive what God had done.

Peter was disembedded from his Jewish boundaries and the Church becomes a previously unimaginable kind of society. Prior to Cornelius, it had been embedded within the ethnocentric cultural world of Israel. Now it becomes something radically different. This was to be a very painful transition. It would cost Peter his life and end, right up to the

present, the Jewish embracing of Jesus. The young church was struggling with her most difficult and deeply felt boundaries.

PAUL

Saul of Tarsus, educated in elite schools, a cross-cultural Jew at
home in the cosmopolitan world of the Roman Empire, could not con-
ceive that the covenant God of Israel was present in Jesus. Saul's zeal for
God outran his contemporaries: *"I advanced in Judaism beyond many
among my people of the same age, for I was far more zealous for the traditions
of my ancestors."*[28] The long-established frameworks of post-exilic,
legalistic Judaism were powerfully embedded in him; they had become
the standard of interpreting tradition for him. Love of the Torah shaped
him. This love made Saul passionate about protecting Jewish life against
any syncretistic encroachments or disloyalty to his interpretation of the
Torah. This drove him to stamp out the new movement of Jesus' followers using every means at his disposal—he felt his actions would obtain
the righteousness of Israel and hasten the day of the Lord.

All of Saul's frameworks blinded him to God's purposes and left
him unprepared for his encounter with the risen Jesus. On the road to
Damascus, his world was radically undermined. The experience literally blinded him, and that blindness was a metaphor for his sudden separation from his world framework and liminality. It was in that state
that this defender of Judaism had to trust the very people who, up to a
moment before, had been his sworn enemies. What emerged from this
liminality and *communitas* was a new man—Paul, the bondservant of
Jesus Christ. Even the leaders of the church in Jerusalem could make no
sense of this transformation. They did not trust what had happened
because it was so far outside their own assumptions about who Saul was.

But, the Spirit of God was creating a continually dislocating and
separating environment for the young church and all its leaders. After
the stoning of Stephen, where Saul stood by holding the coats of the

---

[28] Galatians 1:14

attackers, persecution arose that forced the followers of Jesus out of Jerusalem. Following a basic set of assumptions about what God was creating in the church, the Jerusalem leaders instructed these dispersed Jewish Christians to speak only to other Jews about Jesus wherever they went. But one group broke the boundaries of expectation, crossed into Antioch, and spoke about Jesus to everyone, including Gentiles. The result was massive conversion. The Gospel had jumped the barrier of ethnicity and religious heritage. It was to this multiracial Antioch community, some three years later, that Barnabas invited Paul. There, we see a *communitas* being shaped in a church where race, gender, and ethnicity join with one another. It is from this *communitas* that the call of Paul's mission to the Gentiles emerged.

God Has Not Changed the Pattern

Liminality and transition are not new ideas—they are the documented ways God has been at work through the centuries. These biblical examples show that God has a plan for God's people at all times, though sometimes we must push aside our preconceived ideas and be open for that plan to be in a new place.

REFLECTION AND APPLICATION

1. What new insights into liminality have you learned from exploring these biblical narratives? How do you identify with the senses of separation, loss, and confusion that they experienced?

2. How did God use their sense of separation to bring them into *communitas*? After looking at these stories, what would you add to your definition of *communitas*?

3. What things do you see that can hinder the development of *communitas* in a group of people? How do these happen? How can they be prevented?

4. Look again at these stories and discuss what you feel are the important characteristics of the reformation phase of change. Why was it important that a new generation emerge each time before reformation could truly take place among God's people and according to God's plan?

5. How do you see the Old Testament stories of liminality, transition, and reformation differently from those in the New Testament? What differences did Jesus bring to God fulfilling God's purposes on the earth? What differences did the Holy Spirit bring? How can these help us as we struggle to discern God's mission for our time and live in accordance with it in our times?

TRANSITION
AND CULTURE

Both Liminals and Emergents are struggling to understand how to be the church in a radically changing context. It requires both tribes to discover their need of one another in a *communitas*. However, another component of understanding this is seeing how what is happening in the wider culture also relates to how we lead church systems through discontinuous change.

When a society finds itself in the midst of transition, resistance is as inevitable as it is futile. Most of us resist change when it requires the loss of something deeply important—the rituals and patterns of our lives. The reason we resist is because these rituals and patterns are given to us by the culture in which we are born and formed. Consequently, leading change requires some understanding of the changes taking place in the wider culture.

CULTURE AND SOCIETY

First, we need to distinguish between two related ideas: *culture* and *society*. Anthropologist Clifford Geertz observed that we all begin with the equipment to live a thousand kinds of lives but live only one.[29] The reason for this, said Geertz, is *culture*, which he defines as: "an inherited system of symbolic forms that operates as a set of control mechanisms—plans, recipes, rules, instructions—for governing behaviour."[30] For anthropologist Paul Hiebert, culture is the "more or less integrated systems of ideas, feelings, and values, and their associated patterns of learned behavior and products shared by a group of people who organize and regulate what they think, feel and do."[31] He presents three dimensions to culture: 1) the *cognitive* (ideas), 2) the *affective* (feelings) and the *evaluative* (values).[32] The model below illustrates these levels:

A culture is comprised of all three dimensions. They're the lenses we use to see, understand, and evaluate the world outside ourselves or distinguish our group from others. We produce behaviors and products that express these deeper values (worship, our commitment to the car, our family, a political party, or the type of clothes we choose to wear). Culture represents the core values, ideas, and experiences shaping our perception of the world and gives it meaning. Culture provides us with the symbols, rituals, and narratives that make sense of our lives.

---

[29] Clifford Geertz, *The Interpretation of Cultures* (New York: Basic Books, 1973), 450.

[30] Ibid, 44.

[31] Paul Hiebert, *Anthropological Insights for Missionaries* (Grand Rapids: Baker, 1985), 30.

[32] Ibid, 46.

Society represents the relationships and products we develop to express and give life to our culture. Observable social interactions are what we call *society*. When someone travels abroad and sees the symbol of her nation's flag, it evokes an emotional response that comes from values and beliefs deep within. The flag is an external, surface, social symbol for deeply-held core cultural values.

Obviously, society and culture interact with one another. The primary relationship moves from culture out toward society; the former generates and shapes the latter. Our social interactions are the rich variety of ways we respond to the cultural forces shaping our collective lives.

Hiebert then identifies two levels at which we live: *core* and *surface*. The following simple diagram illustrates this relationship between culture and society.

Surface traits represent what we actually see and experience in society. It is the level of organizations, law, politics, religion, the arts, economics, trends, statistics, habits, the kind of events reported on the news, and the visible artifacts of a society, such as flags, art, and so forth. Beneath this surface level lie the *core* values and frameworks. At the deep center are the *core traits* (worldview) which drive and make a society.

This distinction between the core and surface traits is critical to understanding the nature of the liminality we are confronting. It is also illustrates some of the tension between Liminals and Emergents in terms of the how to address the challenges confronting the church in

North American society. The differences here are about the *levels of change* we have to address, not just in communities of God's people, but in the wider culture within which these communities are located. Societal surface-level issues require one set of skills, but changes in the *core traits* are an entirely different level of change.

The level of change confronting both our churches and our culture are at the level of *core traits*, not simply *surface traits*. As discontinuous change moves us further from the habits and practices that gave stability, the core traits that underlay that societal stability are also increasingly eroded. When this level of change is occurring, our external environments become less and less congruent with the deep-level, inner-organizational patterns and habits we developed to give us identity and meaning as a group or system. The diagram below summarizes this relationship:

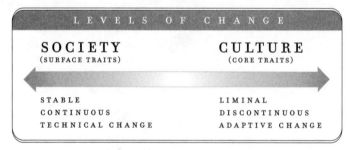

The level of change has shifted from *society* (surface traits) to *culture* (core traits). In this situation, leaders cannot afford to function as if the assumptions of the stability phase are still appropriate, nor is it sufficient to simply react against these assumptions. It is time to form together a *communitas* to discern together ways God is calling forth new forms of life and witness.

LEADERSHIP IN A LIMINAL CULTURE

In the liminal phase of transition the core traits of a culture (either Western culture or the organizational culture of a congregation and denominational system) are changing. This is more than change in popular culture or surface-level changes. By focusing only on these indicators of change, leaders misinterpret what is happening. They will assume their role remains that of managing an organization within the frameworks of their older world. They will shape their responses to discontinuous change on the basis of trends in the popular culture—the surface traits—and so fail to address the deeper issues of core change.

In an earlier chapter we presented this table illustrating the profound levels of change that are currently moving our *culture* through massive discontinuous change.

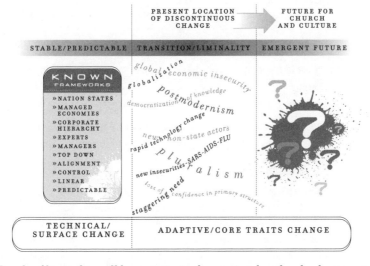

Levels of liminality will keep rising in the coming decades; leaders must learn how to address them. This table illustrates how all of us, Liminals and Emergents, are immersed in core cultural change. No one knows where we are or where we're going. We need each other in *communitas*.

North American culture is in a process of radical change. It is being uprooted in a competition of values as an increasingly globalized, multi-cultural society emerges. At the same time, particular forms of Christian identity are being challenged and disembedded from their former role as a definer of core traits for our culture. This means that most of the change issues the church faces are all shifting to the right side of the chart presented above. The liminality of discontinuous change is happening at levels far deeper than the societal surface with its trends and statistics. It is the core traits themselves that are changing. Basic, long-held, tacit assumptions, frameworks, and values of both our culture and our churches are being challenged, eroded, and transformed.

LIMINALS AND EMERGENTS: ADDRESSING THE CHALLENGES OF CORE TRAIT CHANGE

Edgar H. Schein, in *Organizational Culture and Leadership,* offers six engagements by which Liminals and Emergents might learn how to develop a *communitas* that could address these critical challenges. The following four are directly pertinent to our discussion:

1) *We need to create a common language.* Groups and organizations form their own inner language through which they communicate their core values, ideas, and feelings. The language they use, in turn, contributes to their inner culture. Thus, through trying to determine where they are now and find the best road ahead, both Liminals and Emergents have developed their own languages, and far too often that language separates them (for example the Emergents use the language of *institutional* vs. *organization*). The more this happens, the more difficult it becomes for us to talk with or understand each other. Exclusive and dividing language on both sides creates a simplistic insiders-and-outsiders environment, shutting down the potential of creative and innovative dialogue between groups sharing the same liminality. We are all like this—it is a natural and normal part of the way all social groups function. But in this period of *core trait* transformation, we have to keep the language of dialogue open, not closed. This leads to the second type of engagement that is necessary.

2) *We must redefine group boundaries and criteria for inclusion and exclusion.* Because all groups want to quickly identify who is in and who is out, there needs to be a critical focus on how to

keep the circle of conversation as open as possible. During the long phase of a stable, Christian society, it was relatively simple to establish boundaries based upon certain denominational values and faith statements. These were often based on the formation of the church in post-Reformation Europe and their introduction into North America through differing ethnic groups. Historically, the differentiations of denominational systems were based on this dominant Euro-ethnic division of society. Obviously, after 300 years or more of history, it is not possible to simply dismantle this cultural world in the imagination of people. While it is disappearing rapidly, this world remains alive and its operative functions still shape many church systems. The key here is to find points of dialogue between Emergents and Liminals. There is a need to cultivate open-ended conversations about the nature of the change being faced, and to willingly support each other in experiments for engaging these challenges.

3) *We need to learn to dialogue outside power and status and develop norms of intimacy, friendship, and love.* Liminals and Emergents need new rules of peer relationships. Sharing and openness do not happen by chance, they are a function of carefully worked out, unspoken codes. A façade of cooperation will not do this. This dialogue requires a commitment to get beyond surface conventions to a deeper willingness to meet one another as God's people engaged together in reaching their world with God's mission.

4) *We must get past ideologies.* What this means is that without the ability of leaders to continually step outside the cultural assumptions of their organizations, they will respond to the *core traits* transition of our culture with only the assumptions of *their* group and what has worked for them in the past. This tendency continues in most congregations and denominational systems, but it is also already framing the language and images of the Emergent groups. The internal mechanisms for integration and continuity are very strong. Consequently, Liminals and Emergents approach this transition from within the boundaries of their own frameworks. This new world requires a willingness to reflect on our own ideologies and listen attentively to the ways of others so that they can form a common ground for conversation.[33]

---

[33] Edgar H. Schein, *Organizational Culture and Leadership* (San Francisco: Jossey-Bass, 2004), 70-93.

The challenge is to be able to reconceive our self-understandings in the midst of huge cultural shifts. This involves a rethinking of the culture and frameworks of congregational and denominational life. These are massive challenges. Liminals fear the task of learning new skills and capacities; Emergents keep reacting to the leadership forms they have left behind and are, therefore, less able to appreciate what is present among Liminals than they could be. Leaders on both sides are thrust into a world for which they are ill prepared. The generation who will give concrete shape to new forms of missional life is probably not yet present among us or else is just now entering the dialogue.

IMPLICATIONS FOR LEADERSHIP

Richard Sennett's book, *The Corrosion of Character*, argues that the massive, wrenching changes of the last several decades have had profound consequences for people in the work force of North America that will significantly shape the nature of our culture. He reports on the work life of people in a Boston bakery over a twenty-five year period. At the beginning of that period the bakery was operated by a group of sweaty, somewhat grumpy Greek-Americans. What characterized them was their loyalty to the bakery and their pride of work. These were people invested in their communities.

Twenty-five years later that had disappeared. Machines had replaced these specialists. Transient workers, who spend a few months on the job and then move on, now operate the machines. They are not bakers and have no sense of belonging. They are indifferent and uninvested in what is happening either in the bakery or its neighborhood.[34]

At the other end of the scale, Sennett describes the lives of former IBM executives downsized out of high-paying jobs. The downsizing hit them like an earthquake. By Sennett's account, they had accepted their fate and turned inward; their energy expended in self-awareness, not civic affairs.[35]

---

[34] Richard Sennett, *The Corrosion of Character* (New York: W. W. Norton & Company, 1998), 123ff.
[35] Ibid, 130.

These are radically-changing core values from those that drove our culture half a century ago. Something has shifted. This is a new kind of consensus with profound implications for everyone leading our churches and institutions. We are encountering the responses of people trying to deal with their own liminality. It is a world none of us seem prepared to address.

Leaders must now develop the skills of standing outside their assumed organizational cultures in order to understand the levels of transformation required of them and their systems. They will need to manage the anxiety and resistance that will be a natural response to the notion of entering into a *communitas* with one another. *Communitas* must be based on a dialogue committed to understanding and addressing the discontinuous change in the culture's core traits rather than responding to surface level changes at the societal level.

REFLECTION AND APPLICATION

1. In your own words, define culture and society. How do you differentiate them? Discuss some examples of changes in each in recent years.

2. What would you say are core traits of the Gospel? How are they affected by societal and cultural changes? If the surface traits change, how does that affect these? What is—or should be—at the core of the American church's mission? How can we be adaptive and yet not change our core message?

3. Look again at the chart on page 135. How have these affected our churches? What strengths do Liminals have in addressing these? What strengths do Emergents have? How will *communitas* help us in addressing these?

4. Discuss the four steps Edgar Schein suggests on pages 136-137. How do you see these contributing to a *communitas* of Liminals and Emergents? What are ways that you can facilitate these steps in your congregations?

5. How can we be sure that we are addressing core issues and not just surface issues in our dialogues about transition? How can we be sure to hear a diversity of voices rather than just those similar to our own? Why is this diversity important in trying to form a *communitas?*

SECTION TWO

LEADERSHIP
UNDER A
CHANGING SKY

TRANSITION AND LEADERSHIP

Our next task is to propose a framework for understanding the forces now shaping the church across North America. In summary, to this point I have argued that we are in the midst of a massive transition in which our culture is moving through discontinuous change. One of the outcomes of this larger change is that most of the church systems and leadership capacities that were developed throughout the twentieth century to support the church's role as the religious center of the culture are no longer relevant to leading our churches towards reformation around God's next step for us.

From this set of discontinuities have emerged a variety of programs, groups, proposals, and systems for addressing the church in this time. Among them are two amorphous groupings of leaders and churches: the Liminals and Emergents. The former is largely composed of those whose imagination and leadership skills were formed by the frameworks and practices of the church in last half of the twentieth century. Their experience, world, and loyalties lie with the church systems that flourished in the past. But they also recognize that they are woefully unprepared for either the present discontinuity or whatever the future may hold. They are in a deeply liminal situation because they know that a world has been lost, but have no sense of how to lead or function in the place where they now find themselves.

The Emergents, on the other hand, represent an amorphous collection of younger leaders who have little sense of loyalty to the denominational systems of the past. They are deeply suspicious of the value of the educational systems set up in the twentieth century to prepare leaders for the church and have an almost reflexive reaction to anything they identify as the *institutional* church. But even this group, which views itself at the *experimental* edge of the church's future, is itself in a deeply liminal situation. While it has some fine younger leaders, it is a movement with little sense of how to develop the means for forming its adherents in any way that might produce habits, values, or practices transferable to the future. Emergence is a wonderful concept, but it is far more than simply discussions of postmodernism, the use of technology, or finding new and better ways of addressing forms of life and liturgy from the past.

At the present, these two tribes have little commerce with one another. Yet, the liminal situation in which we all finds ourselves is one that requires the breaking of boundaries, the overcoming of categorization, and a willingness to enter into dialogue with one another without any sense of needing to prove or make the other like oneself. This is what is called *communitas*. In liminality, it is impossible to predict what might emerge. It is a place for listening to one another across tribes and through the gifts each brings to the circle. It is about discerning together some of the skills, capacities, and imaginations that will be required to innovate a missional direction for all God's people. It is a place of both recovering memory and experimenting in new habits and practices. This is why Liminals and Emergents need to find one another in the open dialogue of a leadership *communitas*.

With this groundwork laid, we can now focus on this question of leadership and what might emerge. I believe that as these tribes are willing to come together in local contexts across the barriers, there will emerge among them innovative and creative forms of leadership and experiments that will address the desperate need of the people of God for direction, hope, and imagination. Keep in mind, though, that this is not about a well-laid-out plan; it is about the willingness to engage in *communitas* with one another in the conviction that God's Spirit is among us, and, because of that reality, God's directions and purpose will emerge out of our sincere interactions.

This liminal environment places new demands and stresses upon leaders. It requires a different set of competencies from those in a stable environment. The following chapters propose a number of ways of addressing the leadership issues of a people ready to engage in *communitas*.

CULTIVATING ENVIRONMENTS

The people of God in North America are being called to discern and imagine what it means to be God's missionary people in their own culture. But most people are far from clear about how. The role of leaders is to *cultivate environments that release the missional imagination of the people of God*.

Leadership as cultivation is about creating environments within which God's people shape of their own missional life. This accounting of leadership takes seriously the biblical understanding of the people of God as the place where God's Spirit is most specifically at work. It is in and through God's people that God's future emerges. *Cultivation* describes the essential work of leaders in *communitas*—learning to be cultivators of environments out of which God's people might innovate and imagine where God is at work. It communicates a confidence that in the midst of the liminal, the Spirit is at work forming the future to which God is calling us.

Cultivating leadership does not mean that God's people are simply waiting to suddenly discover the answers to all the problems facing the church. When describing leadership as cultivating environments, leaders protest that this is a simplistic, naïve, and unworkable perspective. Leadership, they argue, is about taking charge, giving direction, and providing vision. In these protests are the deeply-ingrained convictions of modernity about control and predictability. One cannot emphasize enough the depth to which this modern imagination shapes our attitude and evaluation of leadership. The twentieth century was the century of the expert and professional—leadership was functionally and fundamentally removed from the people of God. Leaders were formed in an environment that taught them to believe that they must ultimately have answers, provide solutions, and develop strategic plans. These convictions still lie deep within the imagination of many leaders. As a result, the dramatically-changing environment of our culture and the changed perspectives of younger generations in respect to authority, professionals, and experts creates confusion for these leaders; they feel the conflict between the messages deep inside that have formed them and an awareness that these forms of leadership no longer address the complex, discontinuities of our time.

The issues for Emergent leaders in cultivating these environments are quite different. They too often read notions of cultivation and emergence as a mandate to reject most elements of the forms of leadership that have shaped the immediate past. Some, with instinctive responses to the structured forms of leadership they experienced in their churches, now create new church environments devoid of any kind of leadership, as if there can simply be an unstructured—or anti-structure—form of common life that can be sustained and that represents some new form of being the church in a postmodern world.

Here the understanding of cultivation and emergence is read through the lenses of reactions to the controlling, top-down, professionalization of leadership experienced in former churches or taught in seminary. Emergents have tended to read cultivation and emergence relative to leadership through the *structure/anti-structure* dialectic. As a result, some have gone in the very opposite direction by trying to create contexts in which there is no leadership whatsoever.

Some Emergents move so far from liminal modes of leadership in creating egalitarian or no-leader forms of corporate life that they are unable to recognize some of the important and helpful structures of previous ideas about leadership. There is now an overflow of this reaction. This anti-structure perspective is producing situations where young Emergent leaders, without the benefit of models or mentors, are becoming discouraged and confused by their inability to form enduring community life over the long term. They feel stuck in discussions about elements of community life that could be easily dealt with if there were some basic understandings of structure and leadership as seen by Liminals.

Cultivating leadership recognizes the need for some skilled, experienced people in a community who function like the ancient Abbot/Abbess in monastic communities to nurture younger leaders in skills and practices that have been passed down through the generations and can only be developed through a form of spiritual apprenticeship. This requires a formation of one another as a community of leaders around practices, habits, directions, commitments, and traditions.

Nurturing Teams to Cultivate Environments

Scripture offers a myriad of leadership images. Abraham, Moses, Joshua, Gideon, David, Solomon, Peter, and Paul all functioned out of different roles in radically different situations as patriarchs, judges, elders, kings, priests, apostles, and presbyters. Priestly classes played significantly different roles from those of prophets or poets. Apostles functioned differently from pastors or teachers. At various points in Israel's or the church's history, differing roles had ascendancy and importance.

Throughout Scripture, leadership roles were determined situationally. In the covenant-forming period, it was leaders like Moses and Joshua who rose to authority. As Israel settled in the land among other peoples hostile toward them, judges were raised up and led as they were required. When the economy of Israel switched from nomadic sheepherders to settled city-builders, Israel took on the values and habits of the dominant cultures, and leadership shifted to kings and a priestly class ruling from a centralized capitol and temple in Jerusalem. These leaders became increasingly regulatory, ensuring correct ritual and order. Poets emerged with no formal leadership in the official structures. Their writing expressed a subversive uneasiness with the status quo. They put into language and image the unarticulated longings of minorities for a reframing of Israel's life so that faithfulness to the Lord would again be the standard.

In the midst of acclimatizing to outside cultures, prophets emerged bringing forth words of warning, calling the nation to return to former covenant fidelity. Prophets led from the margins. After 587 B.C., the leadership of prophets came to the forefront as Israel reimagined its narrative and identity in the light of its own liminality. While there were long periods where certain types governed—king and priest in particular—this variety of leadership roles was continually situational.

The New Testament testifies to the struggles of nascent communities of the Spirit working out their identity in diverse, multicultural environments dominated by Greek, Jewish, and Roman structures. The dynamics of this formation were shaped by an accelerating outward thrust from the perceived center in Jerusalem. Yet it was a movement that continually had to address the reality that the church's life was emerging even while it was on the move; it seemed that the central dynamic of its life was a continual uprooting from newly-settled forms of life. It was in constant flux. Order and function had to find a way of living with disruption and emergence. It was a movement being formed along the way. Again, leadership was continually situational and contextual. There was foundational structure—forms of synagogue life provided this structure—but it was also a movement that was continually reframing that structure in the face of ever-changing contextual and situational demands. Structure and emergence walked side by side, not in opposition to one another. This created tension, but it was in the midst of this tension between structure and anti-structure that the missional forms of the people of God took shape.

In these early years, leadership took on diverse roles. Functions were flexible and situational. Roles had little to do with status or regulatory function. They operated through an array of vivid and varied personalities. A list of these leaders would include apostles, evangelists, prophets, teachers, pastors, poets, presbyters, and bishops, among others. But one does not detect, early on, some formal "five-fold" order or pattern that was to be normative for all times and all places. The early communities were situationally shaping leadership out of the context of their own time and experiences, not forming some modern, universalistic patterns that would shape the church for all time. It is only later, as a marginal community is embraced and absorbed into the mainstream of the empire that its leadership functions were gradually reduced to set roles to complement the established patterns and needs of Roman life. These functions are limited to those of pastor/priest/bishop in settled parishes.[36]

During the time of Constantine, leadership roles became shaped by the needs of the social institutions of the empire. The church became alienated from the dynamic of its missional birth and early development. The transformation of its understanding and practice of leader-

---

[36] See Darrell Guder and Lois Barrett, *Missional Church*, chapter 7 for a more detailed overview of this reductionism.

ship has altered the character of Christian identity right up to our own time. Ascetic movements functioned as liminal, anti-structure protests against the developing identity of the church that gradually modeled itself after the vision of the Empire. The Reformation did little to transform these structures; it tended to embed a limited, settled, didactic, care-based, and regulatory practice of leadership. Church leadership was to oversee and regulate the faithful in terms of true word, true sacrament, and true discipline.

This three-fold function of leadership—through word, sacrament, and discipline—dominated the church's self-understanding into the twentieth century. Today, it remains the background against which many denominations still train their leaders. It is this conceptuality and practice of leadership that has run aground, as the church's sponsorship of Western culture has been terminated.

It is this practice of leadership that the Emergents have reacted against, seeking to develop yet-to-be discerned leadership typologies. It is this context that Liminals struggle against—with confusion and a desire to discover alternative forms of leadership. Both tribes seek to reorient their conceptual frameworks. Both are pressed into this liminal place where many of the cultural assumptions of leadership no longer hold. We are all being brought to a place where we must address together our common crisis of liminal identity and discover together the particular ways God would reinvent leadership for this time. To describe the kind of environment in which this might take place, we must briefly examine a different model of leadership and organizational development.

LAWRENCE MILLER'S ORGANIZATIONAL LIFE CYCLES

Lawrence M. Miller identifies a pattern of life stages in the history of organizations.[37] To accompany these, he has also developed a series

---

[37] Lawrence M. Miller, *From Barbarians to Bureaucrats* (New York: Fawcett books, 1990), 2-6.

of leadership typologies. Organizations, he argues, have a life cycle that explains why most decline and die. This cycle provides clues about the nature of leadership at particular points in an organization's life and about breaking the cyclic patterns of growth and decline. Miller argues that the failure of leaders and organizations to address the challenges that confront them is largely a consequence of their failure to understand these stages of change.

Leaders and organizations often fail because they lose connection with the actual changes at work within their organization's culture. They lose their internal power of mission that shaped their initial formation and, therefore, they lose connection with the very groups in the external environment for which they came into being. A vital shift has taken place in the core culture of the organization, a shift that the leadership fails to recognize until it is too late to effectively address it. What is required at this juncture is the formation of a *communitas* between Emergents and Liminals.

Two dynamics are always at work in any organization. On the one side is the outward drive of a vision, a call, and a spirit of passion for that vision and call that drives the organization beyond itself. Then, as success occurs, the organization gradually turns inward to look after its internal world. The focus becomes regulation and identity.

Miller's work goes a long way to explain the current malaise of leadership in church systems, and offers ways in which it might be addressed. He identifies seven stages of organizational life. What follows is a brief synopsis of the leadership types that tend to function in the first six.

1.) **The Prophet** can see and communicate a call to mission. A church formed around this leader has a passionate energy to live into that mission. The prophet is driven by the passion and power of ideas. Detail, implementation, and long-term organizational ability are usually not his or her skills. The prophet is often not equipped with the skills to actualize the vision.

2.) **The Barbarian** is the hardheaded leader willing to implement change, no matter what the price. This is the leader who seizes the moment with single-minded determination. The barbarian takes the vision of the prophet, overcomes obstacles, and turns the vision into reality. The barbarian sees the potential in the prophet's vision and has the capacity to organize and the will do what it takes to turn the dream into reality.

3.) **The Builder** describes a leader who has the specialized skills needed to make an organization grow and develop. While the builder understands the vision, the focus of this leader turns inward. Questions about whether the organization will overcome external challenges and thrive are passing. Now the focus turns to the organization's inner dynamic and the development of infrastructures. At this stage, if the organization's primary leadership remained with the prophet or the barbarian, it would be left in a constant state of vision, crisis, and innovation. Leadership, therefore, switches over to the more inner-directed, builder-leader who shapes the internal ethos, values, and structures. Skills within the organization become more specialized. Process becomes more important. The organization becomes increasingly complex. Attitudes and behaviors change. Role-performance leadership replaces situational leadership.

4.) **The Administrator**. Initially, administration serves the mission of the organization. Gradually, the reverse happens—the organization is shaped by the rules, regulations, and traditions that emerge from within administrative leadership. Holding tradition and the managing regulation dominate. This is the stage when the organization begins its decline. Its ethos is a commitment to order and "following the rule book." The focus of administrative leadership is the managing of the inner life of the system. Administrators believe process is more important than producing the results that engage the organization with its mission. It is when administrate leadership takes over that creative people within the organization begin to look for other places where they can invest their energies.

5.) **The Bureaucrat** is a leader who imposes a tight grip of control over the entire organization. Any who tend toward being prophets or barbarians leave, draining the organization of creativity and mission. The leader is focused on symbols of authority and position rather than the substance of the organization's mission. An entrenched resistance to change exists. Peaceful change becomes less and less a possibility. Problems are dealt with by reorganization. Solutions are sought from within the existing cultural and administrative frameworks. Its culture is based on maintaining the traditional way of life.

6.) **The Aristocrat** merely lives off the system by continuing its ritual life. This ritualized structure carries with it the form and memory of a time when its prophets and barbarians shaped its life, but all substance has long since been abandoned. The aristocrat exists to maintain current function and live off the remaining resources of the system.

These first six leadership roles are illustrated in the diagram below, which depicts the cycle of birth and decline in an organization, and the leadership types that characterize each stage.

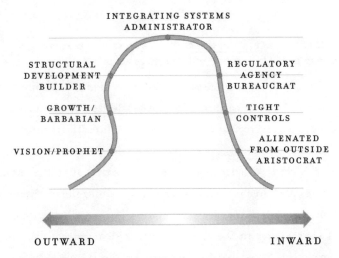

Without some awareness of these dynamics, congregations and denominational systems choose leaders to fit their location in the life cycle rather than leaders who can revitalize them as needed. In practical terms, the probability is that many current leaders in the Emergent tribe, because of their anti-structure orientation, function primarily in the prophetic and growth stages (the left side of the diagram). What is likely absent from the Emergents at this point are leaders with the capacities of builders and administrators who form the systems that make possible the emergence of second and third generations. In contrast, Liminal leaders who have served congregations and denominations for several decades are now in contexts that require prophetic and "barbarian-like" roles—roles which, unfortunately, are foreign to their way of thinking. Younger Liminals find themselves newly entering congregational settings resistant to anything but managers and aristocratic leaders.

If churches are to develop a sustained missional future, the two tribes need to connect. Without each other each, out of its leadership deficits and reactions will form congregations that, a few years hence, will be the mirror images of what currently exists. This would be a tragedy.

A Communitas of Leadership across the Typologies

The role of *pastor* still remains the dominant image of church leadership. For the most part, the role is characterized by administration, care for souls, and regulation of a churched culture. The twentieth century saw the intentional development of this pastor role as a professional with highly-skilled competencies in looking after the internal structures of church organizations and maintaining the traditions and systems that built up over several centuries. The end of the church's cultural sponsorship in the West together with the deconstruction of modernity has conspired to rend asunder the reigning structure of church leadership. This crisis has engendered the current malaise in many denominations and congregations.

The roles of prophet or apostle are largely absent from church systems today. These type of leaders in younger generations increasingly move outside existing church systems, finding no compelling reason to connect their passions with organizational systems dominated by regulation and bureaucratic management. Church systems that remain enclosed within such organizational cultures will be very difficult to turn around.

What can be done? Leaders must cross tribes and discover one another in *communitas*. Within *communitas* is the potential for Liminals and Emergents to discover: a) the power of one another's gifts in leadership; and b) the need to overcome forms of solitary, single-person leadership in forming teams of leaders in communities and geographic areas. Leadership groups must develop and work together across tribal lines as communities. To describe what this means we need to look at the final leadership category Miller develops—the Synergist—and use this descriptor for the recovery of an ancient leadership role—the Abbot/Abbess.

THE SYNERGIST

Miller argues that, if leaders understand the dynamics of organizational change, their systems don't need to move lockstep through the whole cycle and end in death. The key is having an organization that is not defined, or led exclusively, by any one of the leadership roles Miller identifies. The missional vitality of an organization depends on its ability to shape its people around a leadership type he calls the synergist. It is like the role of an Abbot/Abbess: a leader with the capacity to unify diverse and divergent leadership styles around a common sense of missional vision for a specific community. Synergistic leaders call forth a community of leaders of all types—pastor, apostle, teacher, prophet, poet, etc—who, together, cultivate environments that nurture missional life. Such a leadership order can become a *communitas* out of which new forms of missional life might emerge.

The Synergist is a key to this. He/she is capable of incorporating the prophet, pastor, evangelist, poet, and apostle into an order where their skills and insights are equally valid and important. Each has authority as needed situationally in the life of the organization—thus, leadership style becomes situational and shared. The Synergist/Abbot/Abbess creates the social unity that enables this convergence. Certain roles become primary at one time, and secondary at others. The Abbot/Abbess is one experienced and skilled in shaping this order of leaders in the midst of style and role differences. It is this kind of environment that creates the energy and vitality for emergence and innovation.

REFLECTION AND APPLICATION

1. What do you think about this change in leadership from an image as the sole shepherd over the flock who leads where others must follow to a gardener that cultivates missional imagination from the congregation? What forms might this take? How do you see the job description of such a leader changing from pastor to Abbot/Abbess?

2. Look again at the diagram of Lawrence Miller's organizational life cycle. Where do you see your church in this cycle? What leadership attributes do you have right now? What attributes do you need for the present and future of your organization? How will you plug into the leadership styles that you don't have?

3. Describe the role of the Synergist in your own words. How does this leader interact with the other leaders of the life cycle?

4. Describe *communitas* using the terms of Miller's leadership types. Where does each one fit?

5. How do you see a *communitas* of various church leaders in your area working together under the guidance of an order led by an Abbot/Abbess? What attributes and assets are already available to make this type of forum work? Which do you need to develop and strengthen? Are there obstacles that would need to be overcome? What are they and how could you overcome them?

CHAPTER 11

A PROPOSAL

I f the North American church is going to engage our society as a missionary movement to its own culture, then we will need something new to emerge that is not a carbon copy of what has happened in the past. God's future only comes from among from the imagination of God's people. This imagination needs to be released through different kinds of leaders from both tribes as they come together in a leadership order guided by an Abbot/Abbess focused on cultivating a *communitas* among themselves and within their congregations. Such an assembly of leaders is unfamiliar in the Protestant churches of North America. The transformations required to achieve this are immense, but without this change the viability of the church as a missional community is questionable. A major adaptive response to leadership is required.

The need for a movement away from the *sola pastora* ("pastor alone") model of our American church means more than the creation a multitalented staff. It requires rethinking leadership models we have accepted as the status quo. The *sola pastora* identity remains embedded in the church's imagination and practice. Given this, the development and training of an order of missional leaders requires more than traditional seminary programs. Master of Divinity programs are not designed to equip leaders for a missional context. It is based on notions of professionalism out of touch with the information and communications revolutions of the late twentieth century. Emergents grasp this; thus they reject current forms of seminary training even though they are then left with few options for intentional formation. This is why there is a crucial need for orders of leaders in *communitas*. But such orders are never merely spontaneous or leaderless—they require the wisdom, love, and guidance of Abbot/Abbess. Denominational judicatories, congregational leaders, house church groups, Emergent churches, and parachurch groups must join together in a commitment to rethink how we govern and lead our churches.

A Leadership Typology for Transition

The key to such formation is a willingness to yield to the oversight of an Abbot/Abbess. An Abbot/Abbess is someone with the capacity to draw together the energies, diversity, and skills of leaders in the community. Such an integrative Synergist cultivates the spiritual and social environment, which empowers those in the order to operate as a team that takes full advantage of all their different skills. This type of leadership is found in earlier traditions such as Celtic and early monastic orders.

A leadership *communitas* under the oversight of an Abbot/Abbess is difficult to innovate in postmodern, Western societies. The concept of an autonomous self who links with others in contractual relationships lies deep in our lives. At the same time, expressive individualism views any form of commitment or accountability as opening a door to potential abuse and the unhealthy control of the self. The place where these forms of individualism and social contract relationality most deeply have embedded themselves is in North America. Here, the fundamental social commitment is to the self's fulfillment and development and to personal growth and needs, not communal submission and responsibility. Church systems have shaped themselves around these cultural values, self-consciously devising marketing strategies to meet the needs of seekers, rather than engaging holy imagination to discern God's plans and purposes.

We need to break with this *self*-centered imagination of contemporary North American culture, and cultivate of an ethic of commitment and obligation connecting back to older Christian traditions of discipleship and humble apprenticeship. It requires a *communitas* in which each is willing to submit his/her demands for expression to a community shaped by the models of ancient orders guided by an Abbot/Abbess.

In *Reflexive Modernization,* sociologist Scott Lash describes the difference between apprenticeship processes in North America and other countries. He discusses changing environments in modern society wherein the information and communications revolutions have altered the nature and forms of work life. Lash analyzes which systems of formation might best help people to thrive in the globalized environment of the twenty-first century. Surprisingly, it's not in the market-driven individualism of North America, but the more tradition-formed processes of apprenticeship in places like Germany and Austria.

Writing with Lash, Ulrich Beck analyzes the different methodologies for training people in both Germany and the United States. In Germany, until very recently, the norm has been the apprenticing of young people by masters and in schools centered in practical, local, hands-on training. By contrast, in the U.S. such training has tended to be market-driven, highly individualistic, and school-centered in ways that are focused on abstract learning disconnected from actual, local communities in which they can both belong and apply their learning. In Germany, education is based *in the workplace*, where learning is more practical and hands-on. Very little of this kind of teaching is present in the United States. Beck describes the German training and formation in this way:

> The apprenticeship is still based on the *Meistermodell*, reminiscent of medieval guilds, in which workers progress from apprenticeship to journeyman to master. . . . Loyalty and community . . . is in the context of *Beruf*, of the trade or professional community. . . . At issue here is a process not of (reflexive) modernization but of "reflexive *traditionalization*." This is traditionalization in Robert Bellah's sense of an ethics of commitment and obligation, not to the self (which we do see in Anglo-American production systems) but to a *community*. . . . This reflexive traditionalization is not a matter of individualization but one of reflexive *communities* with practices motivated by and oriented to a set of "substantive goods." Such substantive goods are, in Alistair MacIntyre's sense, "internal goods"—that is, not goods external to practices, such a monetary rewards, power or prestige, but goods internal to practices—workmanship or the good of the [community]. These substantive goods also, in Charles Taylor's sense, set themselves off in contradistinction to "procedural goods." In contrast to the procedural . . . ethic [*based on the demarcation of rights and will*] a substantive . . . ethics will be rooted in the *Sittlichkeit* (the ethical life of particular, shared and customary practices) of the . . . community.[38]

It is difficult to imagine the emergence of missional communities of the kingdom without some kind of formation as described here by Beck. The North American church cannot address its malaise and liminality through the forms of training that dominated twentieth-century America. They remain abstractionist and usually fail to address the realities of liminality and transition actually faced in the local context. Our "masters" tend to be men and women with academic credentials

---

[38] Ulrich Beck, Anthony Giddens, and Scott Lash, *Reflexive Modernization* (Stanford, CA: Stanford University Press, 1994), 125-127.

and little connection to the practical forms of experience and knowledge the *masters* have in Germany.[39]

Without an alternative kind of formation, experiments of the
Emergents will peter out after a time because there is nothing to sustain
their ways of life over the long term. At the same time, without this kind
of formation, Liminals will continue to struggle in the malaise of *sola pastora* contexts and professionalized, abstractionist views of leadership.
Together, these tribes have the capacity to find fresh ways of being God's
people, but it requires intentional formation and accountability.
Movements, throughout the church's life, have emerged from such orders
to provide alternative narratives for renewal. This is required again.

There is a space—a new commons of liminality—that makes possible a counter-imagination. In my previous book, *The Missionary
Congregation, Leadership, & Liminality*,[40] a typology of leadership for
liminality and *communitas* was introduced. Four images, or types, of
leadership were described: the leader as *poet, prophet, apostle, and pastor*.[41] This typology argues for a plural, missional leadership team. It
was not presented as an argument for some normative, overarching
leadership type for all time and places, but rather as a helpful way of
recognizing the plurality of leadership God has provided for the church.
Other types could be added to the list, but these were used to illustrate

---

[39] This is not to deny the critical importance of Ph.D. trained teachers. Such people are and always will be
needed. We need excellence in scholarship, but what I want to do here is to raise a basic issue about the
dominant focus of our seminary systems, the type of leaders they are trying to form, and where churches
stand in today's society. Most teachers in seminaries are trained by and for academics—their focus is not
primarily the local congregation. They have been prepared for the kinds of abstract intellectual engagements of academic life and are not really masters who can frame and help form the world of most leaders
who will be serving in the churches across the country. The notion that most of these academics have
served in congregations and know what is going on is disingenuous at best and only serves to cover up a
major problematic in formation. Although it is important to prepare intellectually proficient leaders for the
church, there must also be a reimagining of what training is truly about. Why does formation need to happen by taking people out of their contexts and putting them into abstract, isolated educational modules in
order to prepare them to go back into local contexts? We need something radically different for our social
institutions caught deeply in liminality.

[40] Alan Roxburgh, *The Missionary Congregation, Leadership, & Liminality* (Harrisburg, PA: Trinity Press
International, 1997).

[41] One could have presented further types, such as evangelist or teacher, but the number of types does not
affect the basic argument being made here about the formation of a team of leaders living in and cultivating *communitas*.

the point. This typology is summarized below as a framework for what is being proposed.

THE LEADER AS POET

As a group shifts from stability into discontinuity, its stress and anxiety rise significantly. Two dynamics occur simultaneously. First, the group feels increasingly disconnected from the established, stable traditions and frameworks that gave it meaning. Second, most don't understand and so can't articulate what is happening to them. In this situation, people react to the surface events that are in front of them—a church board reacts to teenagers wearing body jewelry, another group reacts to the introduction to certain styles of music or worship. They don't really know *why* they react the way they do, but react they will.

Before people can move forward, they need to make sense of the experiences that are churning their insides. Leadership at this point is about cultivating an environment that will give voice and meaning to the events that seem to be determining people's lives. This is the work of a poet.

John's prologue begins with its cadent: *In the beginning was the Word. . . . and the Word became flesh and lived among us;*[42] it indicates how the inexpressible identity of Jesus was expressed in human form. The same form of language is used again in his general epistle: *That which was from the beginning, which we have heard, which we have seen with our eyes, which we have looked at and our hands have touched—this we proclaim concerning the Word of life. The life appeared; we have seen it and testify to it.*[43] God's identity and nature are no longer hidden and unknown. In Jesus, God takes off the veil. In a corresponding sense, poets bring forth and make flesh that which is hidden; they take off the veil and give people language to describe what they are experiencing.

Poets listen for the stories, symbols, signs, and language beneath people's words. In traditional cultures, this person was silent much of

---

[42] John 1:1,14.
[43] 1 John 1:1-2 NIV.

the time, listening to the talk of the people and, out of that listening, giving voice to the unarticulated feelings of the people. The poet has need to neither criticize nor judge, only to bring to the surface the voice and soul of the people so they are able to give voice to what they are feeling.

Of course, the poet can only do this as he or she lives deeply within the traditions and narratives of the people—the poet is reflexively living in the traditions. This is what makes the poet so powerful and so essential. The poet's role is to articulate the tradition so that it gives meaning and language to the people's current confusion. Ancient poets would do this through music, story, writing, art, and imagery. Their core skills were the ability to listen to the stories of the dominant, surrounding culture, understand the ways it enters, shapes, forms, and interacts with the community, and unfold what is happening in these currents through their art.

The poet listens to the rhythms and meanings occurring beneath the surface. The poet, therefore, pays little attention to trends, demographics, or the latest programs everyone is buying. The poet will not be caught up by the attractiveness or trendiness of a surface-level world. As John O'Donohue explains it:

> In the postmodern culture there is a deep hunger to belong. . . . Society is losing the art of fostering community. Consumerism is now propelling life towards the lonely isolation of individualism. Many of the keepers of the great religious traditions now seem frightened functionaries; in a more uniform culture, their management skills would be efficient and successful. In a pluralistic and deeply fragmented culture, they seem unable to converse with the complexities and hungers of our longings. From this perspective, it seems we are in the midst of a huge crisis of belonging. When the outer cultural shelters are in ruins . . . the recognition of our hunger to belong may gradually assist us in awakening new and unexpected possibilities of community and friendship.[44]

---

[44] John O'Donohue, *Eternal Echoes* (New York: HarperCollins, 1999), xxiv-xxv.73

A poet's leadership expresses itself in several directions at the same time. First, the focus is on the people: the questions, issues, and confusions shaping their lives. The poet listens to the rhythms: the stories, events, symbols, and values that combine in a variety of ways to form who we are. Most of the time, most of us are unaware of these rhythms; they are the background sounds and images we overlook. They are memories that form us and, often, the memories we have forgotten or think are meaningless. When this happens, the very memories that were meant to give ballast and compass to our lives are lost, so that in times of disruption, we feel lost and confused because the narratives we think we understand no longer seem to sustain or give life. They seem to be pulling us apart, becoming contradictory and dissonant. The result is increasing levels of stress and confusion. People find it increasingly difficult to make sense of their world. Here is the pain, anger, and confusion of liminality.

Thus we need to return to these narratives and gain new insight. Poets are the ones who can reframe these narratives to give us that new insight. Poets aren't strategists with solutions or answers. They give language out of the tradition and its memory so that people develop awareness and begin to dialogue about their current experiences.

Furthermore, poets immerse themselves in the multiple stories running beneath the surface of the culture. They feel the power of these stories and critique their claims and pretensions on the basis of the memory and tradition of the community. The poet is deeply embedded in the memory and tradition of the Christian story and has the gift of getting inside the ways a particular community of Christians has become integrated into the wider culture's values and ideologies.

Part of the liminality experienced in Christian communities is that they have lost the sense of the Christian story among all the ideologies swirling about in their postmodern culture. They have little memory and few frameworks with which to discern the difference between the

Christian narrative and competing stories that seem to reside in grayness of meaning.

Poets discipline themselves to see the world differently from most. They are not so much advice-givers as image- and metaphor-framers. One of the crucial needs of the liminal situation of Christian communities is for people to discern the shape of the captivities that have overtaken us. What the churches need are not more entrepreneurial leaders with wonderful plans for their congregation's life, but poets with the imagination and gifting to cultivate environments within which people might again understand how their traditional narratives apply to themselves today.

So many of the programs on church health can only lead the churches down more of the same utilitarian and technological dead ends that have contributed to its current malaise. Poets are leaders for our time who evoke the words and images that disclose the captivity in which we are enmeshed—they provide us with the environments in which we might develop awareness and understand our situation.

Walter Brueggemann describes our liminal situation well:

> The loss of that world . . . is enormously frightening and disturbing . . . our fear invites us to gestures of nostalgia, and it reduces us to acts of brutality . . . our culture is one in which an old imagined world is lost, but still powerfully cherished, and in which there is bewilderment and fear, because there is no clear way on how to order our shared imagination differently or better.[45]

Ours is a deeply dislocated society in which the old certitudes, privileges, and dominations are ineffective, frayed, and fragile. Our lives are experienced as the torn fabric of an old, well-worn coat that no longer protects from the elements. The threads of individualism, technique, materialism, and autonomy wove this fabric. This became the story that really dominated our lives and caused the biblical narrative to fade from

---

[45] Walter Brueggemann, *Texts Under Negotiation* (Minneapolis: Augsburg Fortress Publishers, 1993), 19.

memory. Therefore, we have little capacity to discover the resources that might bind our lives together and provide new clothing. Many in our churches are bewildered; they are seeking only ways to survive in a seemingly hostile environment. This is a hard situation for people. Denial and despair, coupled with a powerful, nostalgic desire to recapture the past, increasingly form people's responses. This is where the poet's skills are most needed. As Eugene Peterson points out: "Poets draw us into deeper respect both for words and for the reality they set before us."[46]

The poet's heart is shaped by the question: How may we cultivate an environment that helps us see our experiences and context through the eyes of the tradition and its core narratives? Brueggemann views the poet's means of doing this as hinting, painting pictures, and creating imaginations that run counter to the dominant ideologies. Poets give language that assists the community to discern itself amidst the perplexity, confusion, and despair that comes with the loss of a world and framework.

At the same time, poets make available a future that does not exist as yet; they are eschatologically oriented. From this environment, a missional imagination emerges. The poet does not provide outlines for action or detailed pictures of that future, but creates a metaphor, story, image, liturgy, and imagery to point toward an open-ended hope. In this way the poet invites the community into dialogue about its current experiences and that dialogue is shaped by memory and eschatology.

Poets have been given little attention in the churches of modernity. They have been considered somewhat odd secondary persons who bring aesthetic engagement, but are not crucial to the real work of making the church an effective instrument of growth. Even to this time, the majority of leaders in the churches remain convinced there's a rational strategy, a technique, or a plan that will define a preferable future and bring it into the present. People want the poet to be practical and useful, but poets don't bring solutions, they ask questions that invite dialogue and

[46] Eugene Peterson, *The Contemplative Pastor* (Grand Rapids: Eerdmans, 1989).

undermine previous assumptions. The poet knows that only in this questioning and dialogue is it possible to be the community of God's future that discovers along the way its forms of missional life.

Poets are usually not concrete, solution-driven people. Their tools are words, metaphors, stories, and symbols. These tools have fallen into misuse in an age of technique, quick fixes, and how-to books. The feeling seems to be that if it isn't immediately usable, then it has little value. This is because the congregation is also seen as a tool that is to be used to make something happen. But the poet knows that the congregation is not a tool—it is the location where God's work of redemption in Jesus and the eschatological future of the kingdom become present in the lives of God's people.

Poets cultivate the imagination of an alternative world. Consequently, their language is often ambiguous. Poets trust that God takes these words—the biblical stories, the questions, images, and metaphors—and, in God's own time, uses them to reshape the imagination of the community into new directions. They create an environment of story and questions that invites God's people to articulate their experience of the loss of a world and begin to hear the possibilities of alternative imaginations and futures.

The poet's work is only a part of the work of leadership. He or she longs to care for and watch over the people of God, but is also deeply committed to engaging people in both the narrative memories that give identity and the possible future that God has for them.

THE LEADER AS PROPHET

Alongside the poets, there are the prophets, whose focus and desire is that the people of God rediscover the Word of God. They want to reform the common life of God's people around faithfulness to God's unfolding story. While poets invite dialogue in awareness and understanding, prophets call people to act on that knowledge. Liminality is the rich soil of prophetic imagination. It provides an environment where people are aware that they've lost their world and the connection with their most determinative stories. Prophets know that this loss of story is a huge obstacle to the recovery of a missional life. They seek to address this social and theological reality.

The prophetic desire is to lead God's people into a reengagement with God's story. This is a narrative that is far different and larger than the current focus on the expressive individual—the self of modernity. It is radically different from some needs-centered message about how God will make our life work if we as individuals just make the right kinds of commitments. The prophet understands that the sources of such are unformed, un-catechized communities of the kingdom who have lost the ability to recognize the alternative story that lives in the Bible. The work of centering Christian community within God's story is the enormous task the prophet desires to shape in order to form such communities as a sign, witness, and foretaste of God's reign.

The exile of Israel in Babylon that we discussed in some depth illustrates this prophetic role. In 587 B.C., the Babylonians descended upon Jerusalem, tore down the walls, destroyed the temple, and seemed to crush what remained of the Davidic monarchy. It was a devastating, world-ending event in the life of Judah. Captives were deported to Babylon, where they sat by the river and wept as they remembered Zion. They could not sing the Lord's songs in a strange land. The prophet Jeremiah explains why this happened—they had left Scripture to accept their own distorted version of God's story for them. In their story, God would keep Judah and Israel—city, temple, monarchy, worship practices—intact and protected from all enemies no matter what because they were God's special, chosen people. It wasn't the true story of God's desires or purposes found in Scripture, but a constructed myth.

During the seventy years of exile, people were confronted by the painful reality of the myth's failure and their own incapacity to faithfully live out God's story. In those years the exiles had to reenter God's true story all over again. This time they read and heard God's story from a radically different place—the place of loss, confusion, and despair of a world that had ended and a framework that had failed them. This was the central work of the prophets in exile—to reconnect them with God's true story for them.

In exile/liminality, the prophet does not develop strategies for returning to the past, but cultivates an environment that helps people reengage with God's narrative. The prophet's story-recovering role is shaped by the impulse to form a people who engage their contexts from the perspective of God's story. In this sense, the prophet, like the poet, indwells the tradition, but also points to its eschatological reality in the call to live out the present. Prophets understand that the tradition must be appropriate in the present. As the poet calls people to an articulation of their pain and loss, the prophet pushes them toward a vision of how and where God is shaping them at the moment. The poet gives language to people's experience; the prophet brings them back to the words of the narrative, addressing people with the decisions and direction of the Spirit's future.

Prophets reconnect people with the meaning and actions of God's radical call out of the past and invitation into the present practices of the eschatological Spirit. In our time the gospel has been reduced to values and morals, to aesthetics and spiritual experiences. Because of this, it is difficult to encounter the God of Scripture. Ecclesial life is not about the formation of a missional community, but the formation of the church as an instrument for marketing religious goods and services. Only by reinhabiting its foundational stories in Scripture and tradition can the church comprehend and encounter God's story. The prophet creates situations that compel the community to do just that.

Prophets announce the presence of the eschatological future of the Spirit among the people. It is this presence of the future in the Spirit that creates new social possibilities in a world of crisis. Isaiah declares: *"Behold, I am doing a new thing,"*[47] addressing a people consumed with their old world, sitting in self-pity, loss, and confusion. It is a declaration of imagination and hope, spoken when there were no markers on the horizon to substantiate the announcement. The prophet discerns a world almost no one else sees.

The poet's primary concern is *for the people* and the desire to inspire in them new insight. The prophet's concern is giving tangible expression to *what God is saying* to the people. While the prophet may speak in the language of the poet, the drive is not primarily comforting the *people of God*, but expressing the *word of God*. Each has its place and legitimacy.

The prophet is given for the in-between time of liminality, not to change the world, but to resist the reductionism of the world in the community of Jesus and to point to a different way of being that community. In the midst of Israel's exile, Isaiah announced unbelievable words: *"Your God reigns!"*[48] It expressed an alternative story about what was happening in their world. If the poet works at getting people in touch with the anxieties and pain of their time and place, the prophet calls back into memory the story of God's presence. The prophet works at living faithfully into that story. At the center of the prophetic perspective is this odd and passionate need to articulate a world in which God is at the center of the story, not our own human identity.

THE LEADER AS APOSTLE

Apostles have a clear sense of calling, mission, urgency, and direction. They hear the voices of the poet and prophet and set about to make what God is saying through them a reality. Judah did not remain in exile; out of the liminality emerged leaders with new vision for God's plan. The apostolic function is to lead God's people into the *missio dei*—the "mission of God." Apostles stand at the doorway between an old world

---

[47] Isaiah 43:19 ESV.
[48] Isaiah 52:7.

that has died and the transition world that lies ahead and calls people to action. One of the great gifts of the missional conversations of the past decade is a recovery of the understanding that the church, in all its forms, is fundamentally *apostolic* in nature.[49]

Whatever emerges in terms of new forms in the years ahead, a missional church will have at its center an apostolic identity and an apostolic leadership. An apostle is a leader who thoroughly understands the crisis through which we are moving, and grasps the kinds of actions that must be taken in order to engage the community of God's people with the *missio dei*. This is a leader who can turn dreams into deeds. Like a building constructed according to a blueprint, the apostle longs to turn outlined images and dreams into concrete reality.

What we mean by apostle here is *not* the modernity image of the strong, entrepreneurial leader who has a plan and program for people and leads them in that direction with some form of strategic plan. The apostle is not the super-hero figure who comes in to rescue helpless people with God's plan for the future that has been revealed to him or her. This is modernity at work with its inner conviction that with the right individual, the right plan, and the right actions we can control the world and shape our own preferable future. This is not what we mean by apostle! It is so easy to fall into this modernity myth because people are anxious to find someone with all the answers and all the plans. This is still a powerful and virulent myth in our culture. However, the true apostle understands these key elements:

> » God's Spirit is among God's people (the ordinary men and women in local gatherings).
>
> » Therefore, *God's future* is among God's people, not in some individual leader's plan.
>
> » The role of leadership is to create environments that release this missional imagination of the people of God so that they can discover God's plan and put it into action in their local contexts.

---

[49] See Robert J. Scudieri, *The Apostolic Church* (St. Louis, MO: Lutheran Society for Missiology, 1995).

The apostle does not come to people or communities saying: "Here's what God has shown me about what we should do as a community and here's the plan for doing it!" On the contrary, the apostle says to the people: "We know we have been called to be the sign, witness, and foretaste of the kingdom. We know we are called to be the sign of the *missio dei* in this community. So here is how we can act on what God is saying, forming, and calling forth among us!"

This apostle's passion and single-minded focus on turning God's community into a people of action around the *missio dei* can make them threatening to people. Church systems have tended to push such leaders out because of fear and their inability to control such leaders. Apostles, even more than prophets, threaten the culture of the organization because they push for action and can articulate how that action might happen. Furthermore, the apostolic gift has hardly been recognized in the pastor-dominated paradigm of leadership. It is, therefore, difficult for those with apostolic gifts to understand their impact within pastor-dominated systems.

Apostles are often intuitively aware that current structures and frameworks no longer sustain a relevant encounter of the gospel with the culture. But this often gets heard as a negative criticism of the institutions and the people who run them. They are, therefore, perceived as threatening by those within church systems of all kinds and are pushed to the margins of such organizations. At this moment in time, we need to discover the apostolic gifts all over again, granting them affirmation and legitimacy.

The apostle builds on the work of the prophet by forming environments that empower people to engage their communities and contexts in terms of *missio dei*. Apostles can envision and implement practical ways to live out God's narrative in this time and place. The apostle brings to leadership a practical focus on the outward journey of engagement with the culture. The single-mindedness of this passion can be disconcerting, but it also creates an environment wherein God's people practice the *missio dei*.

But the apostle isn't simply outer-directed and action-orientated. This leader can theologically and ecclesiastically filter the lived context of a community through the lens of the gospel and shape environments that release people into missional life. They are passionate in their commitment to action. People are drawn to them because of their conviction and energy. Apostles embody an unshakable faith in God's emerging future among the people. What makes them different from prophets is the ability to form practical ways for the community to implement the visions and directions the Spirit is calling forth. The apostle turns his or her energies and passion to continually moving God's people out into their varied expressions of the *missio dei* in that context. In this sense the apostle tends not to manifest pastoral gifts. The heart to care pastorally is present, but the drive toward *missio dei* is primary.

Paul is an obvious example of an apostle. His letters to the young churches show a great tenderness. The pastoral heart is there, but what is primary is the focused drive and the single-minded attention to the missional task set before him. His confrontation with Barnabas over John Mark's ability to participate effectively in the missionary band is an example of this focus. While Barnabas was focused on Mark, seeing what the young man would become, Paul was driven by the immediate need of the task at hand. He wanted competent people about him who could take direction and get on with the mission. It is this apostle-leader who transforms organizations from inward-focused bureaucracies to vital mission outposts.

When an organization is stuck in its own interior life or confronted with the crisis and chaos of liminality, the apostolic leader is an essential member of any leadership team. In the twentieth century, churches moved into management/bureaucratic care-giving styles of leadership.

The emphasis was on managing the system and caring for the people who came as members. There are now few within these systems with memory or capacity for apostolic leadership. Such leaders have tended to move outside these systems (joined the Emergent tribe) and, hence, function on their own without the appropriate gifts and meliorating capacities of the other leadership types.

At the same time, the Liminals within denominational systems are without the gifts and energies of apostles. Prophetic-apostolic leadership, so essential in this phase of transition for existing denominations and congregations, continues to be drained off into alternative movements that will allow them the scope to express their gifts. The tragedy is then that there is an absence of the prophetic-apostolic skills, gifts, and memory necessary to sustain and deepen their lives.

To a large extent, the apostolic leaders critical for the reinventing of a missional identity are still being formed. They are not likely to be located among the current leaders of liminal churches, but there are hopeful signs. In the United Kingdom, Anglicans and Baptists have joined together in a wonderful cooperative experiment called *The Order of Mission*, which is equipping and forming a younger generation of leaders. This exciting development focuses around shared leadership and formation based upon missional practice in local communities. God's Spirit is at work cultivating alternative forms of missional life through an immensely innovative and generative process of leadership formation.

THE LEADER AS PASTOR/TEACHER

It may seem strange to place this most well-known leadership type last. It has been the primary and almost only form of church leadership for almost two millennia. The Reformation didn't address or change this form of leadership, but shifted some of its functions from priest to teacher/care-giver. Following the Enlightenment, the pastoral role became more deeply embedded in the imagination and practice of Western Christianity. Friedrich Schleiermacher, addressing the "cultured despisers" of Christianity, redefined the pastoral role in terms of an educated professional.[50] Professionalization, of one sort or another, has been the continual response ever since. This professionalization in its multiple forms as therapist, CEO, spiritual director, and provider of religious goods and services to seekers or members has driven the critique of Emergents.

With the exception of emerging experiments in the United Kingdom and some places in North America, however, there still remains an inability to imagine leadership other than *sola pastora*. It is not possible to cultivate missional communities of the kingdom based on this leadership form. Missional communities that engage the constant change that lies ahead will need to transform congregational, denominational, and educational paradigms of leadership. Pastoral leadership can function as the primary role identity of leaders only within long periods of cultural stability. We are far from such a period at the moment. This does not mean the pastoral role is unimportant. It remains essential; but it must be seen in relationship to the other leadership types and not as the sole type of leadership to be desired.

CULTIVATING A COMMUNITAS OF LEADERS

In summary, here are some principles for forming a *communitas* of leaders:

1) Leaders are required from both tribes and across varying typologies who meet each other in a new kind of commons.

2) The central purpose and imagination of the *communitas* is the formation of *local* missional communities across church and denominational boundaries. This is why referring to it

---

[50] Friedrich Schleiermacher, *On Religion: Speeches to its Cultured Despisers* (Louisville, KY: Westminster John Knox Press, 1994).

as an *apostolic* network of leaders is appropriate. It doesn't mean all need apostolic gifts, but that the apostolic heart of witness and mission controls the work and vision of the network.

3) Because such a *communitas* is formed from among both Liminals and Emergents, leaders will bring with them some of the polity, structural, and organizational forms of their church cultures (ex: positional leadership, requirements of denominational bodies). These cannot be denied, but must become secondary to the task of forming a *communitas*.

4) The varying gifts and types are the ingredients of a leadership *communitas* and as such need to be allowed to operate freely as part of what binds the team together.

5) Alongside the singular, stand-alone congregation that characterizes Protestantism, we need to cultivate experiments wherein leaders in a geographical area are formed into an apostolic network to co-serve multiple congregations, house churches, and other forms of missional witness.

6) The four leadership gifts illustrated above (together with others such as evangelist and teacher and so forth) will interact with one another in a *communitas* that seeks to understand and address the adaptive challenges of the *missio dei*. At particular times, certain types will provide primary direction, but always under the overall direction of the Abbot/Abbess.

7) This leadership *communitas* will require a willingness to allow a mixed economy of structures and systems. In some locations, for instance, a group of congregations, house churches, and others might form themselves around such a local leadership *communitas*. Such mixed economy systems are appropriate when the key is experimenting and co-learning.

8) A fruitful and generative context in which to develop such mixed economy experiments is between Liminals and Emergents. As the church groups in each of these tribes cross boundaries, letting go of reactive responses to institutional churches or postmodern experiments, it will be possible to form experiments in which all participate.

9) Leadership in *communitas* is neither positional nor hierarchic (although such forms will return in the future—there is nothing inherently wrong with appropriate hierarchy).

10) A leadership *communitas* requires a synergistic interrelationship between the various gifts in order to function. This does not happen by chance but requires the presence of a leader with the oversight and wisdom to guide the work of such a network. This leads to the introduction of one final, but critical leadership type—the Abbot/Abbess.

REFLECTION AND APPLICATION

1. How would you describe the Synergist or Abbot/Abbess? What would the job description for such a person look like? What type of personality and leadership attributes would such a leader need?

2. What do you think of the apprenticeship model as described by Beck, Giddens, and Lash on pages 161-163? Do you think this is a good model for our churches to follow or is it lacking in some areas? How would our sense of expressive individualism need to change for us to fit into such a framework?

3. What does this apprenticeship model do to build community? How can we capture the best elements of this to put them to work in our local churches and regions? What are those best elements?

4. Discuss the leadership gifts of the poet, prophet, apostle, and pastor/teacher. How do you see these interacting with the leadership types of the prophet, barbarian, builder, administrator, bureaucrat, and aristocrat as discussed in the last chapter? Where do they overlap? Where are they different? Are all of the different types necessary to a living, growing church organization?

5. How do you see the system proposed here differently from the *sola pastora* model that most churches have followed for the last several centuries? What changes need to be made in your church to get closer to the model proposed here? How could such changes come about with drastic reactions to the changes? What might your *communitas* of leaders look like for your congregation?

THE ROLE OF THE ABBOT/ABBESS

The role of the Abbot/Abbess goes back into the traditions of the church's missional life. The term itself has connotations of male primacy—*abba* is from the Syriac form of the Hebrew meaning "father"—but in Celtic monasticism, up to the Council of Whidbey, women served equally in this role as Abbesses. In the role of an Abbot/Abbess are resources for the formation of missional leaders and missional communities.

Historically, Abbots/Abbesses provided oversight to a community of monks/nuns in *orders* formed around a way of life. The Abbot/Abbess formed an extended contrast society of the new family in Christ whose characteristic way of life was not power or control, but self-giving love. What shaped their life was an *ideal* rooted in Jesus and the *missio dei*. In the Celtic context they were not cloistered communities, but families extending outward in the *missio dei*.

An important key to the leadership *communitas* discussed in previous chapters is the role of such an Abbot/Abbess. It is not a new role. Benedict's Rule explains that the role of an Abbot/Abbess is: *"to care for*

and guide the spiritual development of many different characters."[51]
The primary roles of Abbot/Abbess we want to lift up are:

> » **The formation of a witnessing community of love shaped around the ideal of the new family; an extended gathering of assorted people in Jesus.** This kind of community lives in contrast to the dominant use of family language in many congregations where it functions to protect a narrowly-defined, bounded group comprised mostly of a homogenous, socio-economic class huddling together against difference and strangers. The notion of a community of love as a witnessing family in the world is very ancient; it goes to the core of Christian identity as the Spirit-filled society among those from whom God's future emerges.

> » **The ordering of common life around the *Opus Dei* or "work of God."** Here the Abbot/Abbess' role is to direct the life of the community around God's purposes. This is a different work than that of therapist and caregiver to expressive individuals or a CEO with a strategic plan. It is about the formation of people involving attention to structure and catechesis.

> » **The oversight of the various works, mission, and activities of the community.** This would be especially the case in terms of being able to synergize the various energies and tensions that are a normal part of any community.

LEADERSHIP, TEAM, AND TRANSITION

This leadership *communitas* under the guidance of an Abbot/Abbess is more than an add-on to current congregational leadership. Questions about how to add this on to what leaders are already doing or about adding more staff to create a team miss the point. What is being proposed is a different perspective. The malaise of the church cannot be addressed through adjustment; it requires a change in the nature of

---

[51] Anthony C. Meisek and M.L. del Mastro, *The Rule of Benedict* (NY: Doubleday/Image Books, 1975).

leadership. Liminals and Emergents in a geographic area shape together experiments in the formation of a leadership *communitas* to the development of missional communities. What would this look like?

In a city or town, a combination of congregations, church plants, and house churches would form a common leadership *communitas* under the direction of an Abbot/Abbess. It functions for all the communities to cultivate environments that call forth missional life in, among, between, and across the groups. This *communitas* is comprised of the various leader types outlined above working on behalf of the *missio dei* among the communities. They function as a *missional order* called to the task of leadership in that area. The following diagram illustrates the overall picture.

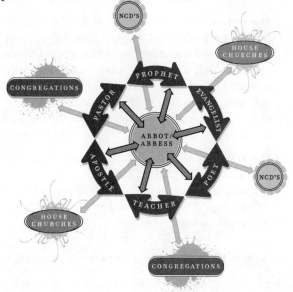

The Abbot/Abbess is not a denominational executive carrying out the policies and procedures of a denomination. The role is to oversee and guide the leadership *communitas* in its work. The *communitas* is a missional order composed of men and women committed to the *rules* of that order. Some of those rules would be:

» A commitment to place—the geographic area/neighborhood—rather than just the congregation, house church, or New Church Development (NCD).

» Keeping the Daily Office as a community, which is the appropriation of the practice of a community to stop at various times in a day for prayer, silence, reading Scripture, and basic confessions of the faith.

» Commitment to the oversight and authority of the team by the Abbot/Abbess.

» The order will be focused on discerning the forms of the *missio dei* in the various worshipping communities.

» Callings and gifts will be shared for the sake of the whole rather than any specific group within the overall community of believers.

We get a glimpse of this kind of leadership community in Acts 13 where the church in Antioch was comprised of a wonderful assortment of leaders working skillfully together. Though this passage of Scripture doesn't provide a detailed picture, we do see a diverse group gathered around the practices of prayer and discernment for the sake of the church in the whole city and region. We know, at least, that there was a pastor and apostle in the team—Barnabas and Paul—as well as certain prophets. One suspects there were also teachers and poets in the group. They came together for the church in Antioch, not just one specific congregation or experiment.

LIVING COMMUNITAS AND MISSIO DEI

If this proposal sounds new, it is because we have lost the memory and experience of how the church framed itself in other missional contexts. However, this memory exists in many of our scriptural and traditional narratives. We need to recover this memory and channel it into fresh imagination and new risks for the kingdom.

A lot of congregations, house churches, and New Church Developments (NCDs) tend not to have the leadership types they need among themselves. The result is a continuing cycle of decline, discouragement, and burnout among emerging experimental churches and a large percentage of NCDs that fail to flourish. The crisis is not just discouragement among existing leaders, but a rapid loss of small, local congregations rooted in neighborhoods where they can live an incarnational life in context. Just as Wal-Mart models suck up the small neighborhood stores resulting in weaker social and economic links in a community, the loss of small, local churches to the regional, megachurches is an equally great tragedy for the missional life of the church. We need a new imagination about being the church in, for, and with local neighborhoods and communities.

This presents significant challenges, but that is the nature of a liminal context. A missional order of Emergent and Liminal leaders in local contexts could address many of these challenges, calling forth the imagination of God's people in experiments of missional engagement. In each church group there would be a leadership team (these are already in place in the form of boards, sessions, etc.). The leadership *communitas*, under the direction of the Abbot/Abbess, would assign one of its members to a congregation, house church, or NCD; but there would the opportunity to provide the multiple skills of the whole team to these contexts. The potential for teaching, preaching, training, and equipping is multiplied enormously. The resources of the numerous communities become available for one another in the common work of the *missio dei*. On regular occasions the churches in the area would come together for worship, celebration, story telling, and training so that no small community is alone in its journey. Because the leadership *communitas* is itself formed as a missional order it models how each community can be formed.

Numerous church systems already have elements of such forums in their polities, but to a large extent their sense of missional imagination has been displaced by regulatory structures—administrators and bureaucrats have taken the leadership from prophets and apostles. In Presbyterian governance, for example, the pastors of local congregations are not ordained to the local church but to the Presbytery of their city or region. This reflects the faint memory of a way of formation and accountability for the whole city or town that is largely forgotten. Most Presbyterian pastors, like their congregations, are moving rapidly away from a way of life actively connected to their communities into a form of congregationalism focused merely on their own congregations. Presbytery executives now operate as managers of polity rules and regulations, rather than as Synergists (Abbots/Abbesses) of missional leadership for the sake of the *missio dei* in that Presbytery.

The precedents for this proposal go back a long way in the church's history. In the post-apostolic period, the church in a city was comprised of a series of house churches, or larger gatherings, connected to each other through a bishop and group of elders who provided oversight and training for the house churches. Augustine, as Bishop of Hippo, operated in this way. As Bishop he had oversight of the *church* in Hippo (note the singular) which was comprised of a small numbers of people who gathered in households. A group of elders (presbyters) worked as a team in the care and training of these smaller groups.

In some of the earlier monastic orders, similar structures emerged. In Ireland, after Patrick, an Abbot/Abbess of emerging communities shaped the overall life of people who saw themselves as both a gathered church and a missional band commissioned to demonstrate and announce the gospel. Within these missional communities were gifted leaders who functioned under the direction of the Abbot/Abbess. We have a rich reservoir of images and resources from the church's own history to help us engage the leadership challenges of today.

It's not possible to jump straight into the forming of such leadership communities—a lot of groundwork is first required. Dialogue is needed between Emergents and Liminals in an area. Different formats for these gatherings need to be developed and experimented with to fit particular contexts. Abbots/Abbesses need to found, trained, and empowered. An apprenticeship/discipleship program is needed. Efforts towards communitas need to be documented, researched, and reviewed to analyze what is being learned and develop new instructional resources for this leadership method. However, the imagination to engage in this work is already present across the church—we need a willingness to risk and experiment. In many places such experiments are presently in process—in *The Order of Mission* in Sheffield, England; at Southside Church in Vancouver, Canada; and in Eagle, Idaho near Boise. A training center—The Allelon Center for Missional Leadership[52]—is already being formed to train and equip leaders for these kinds of missional communities.

One can imagine five to ten congregations, house churches, and NCDs coming together and bringing Liminal and Emergent leaders into this process. Some denominational leaders, seminary educators, and key leaders in the emergent churches could call together leaders into an experiment that forms a band of missional leaders and churches for an area. These leaders might make a five-year covenant with one another, find an Abbot/Abbess, and check into the training resources of The Allelon Center for Missional Leadership as it has already gathered some of the most advanced trainers and research to provide training in this field.

It's Time to Come Back Together

In our times of transition, Liminals and Emergents need each other more than ever before. I firmly believe this is what God is calling us to in our times.

---

[52] For more information on this Center, check out its website at *www.allelon.org*

Through our discussions in this book we have explored the nature of the Liminal/Emergent dichotomy that has developed in our churches today, as well as the phases and characteristics of the discontinuous change we all face. But my hope is more than just a greater understanding of where we are today; my hope is that leaders can put aside past differences and come together in *communitas* in both local communities and local churches so that we can live the missional imagination God will give us through such humility and unity. I feel that the best way to start is to begin missional orders—which contain all of the leadership types working together as a team—under the direction of an Abbot/Abbess as outlined in the last two chapters.

Now it is time for action on the local community level. I urge you to start the dialogue in your area. Contact the Allelon Missional Leadership Network and let us know what you are doing and how we might encourage you. I pray you experience God's best as you strive to live God's mission for your congregation and community.

Reflection and Application

1. How crucial do you see the Abbot/Abbess to this group? How might you find such a person in your area?

2. How large of a geographical area do you think would be practical for your community? In some rural areas this could be tens of miles, for some urban areas tens of blocks. Is there a defined area or region that could set your initial boundaries? What organizations in your area could you plug into for your leadership communitas? Where might your "Daily Office" be located?

3. What gifts and callings do you have in your congregation that you could share with others? What gifts and callings could you pull on from elsewhere to fill gaps or weaknesses in your church? Can you break these needs into categories according to the leadership gifts and types we discussing in the last couple of chapters?

4. What other models for your local *communitas* might you follow in addition to the one in Acts 13? They centered on prayer. How would prayer fit into your leadership order? What other disciplines, practices, and resources would you want as foundation pillars of your order?

5. How would you see such a leadership order working in your community? Would it be something you needed to first start in your local congregation, or are there other area churches you feel you could team up with to start such a forum? How could you start such an order in the next three months? Who do you need to contact? What would you need to do?

BIBLIOGRAPHY

Bauman, Zygmunt. *In Search of Politics*. Palo Alto, CA: Stanford University Press, 1999.

Beck, Ulrich. *Democracy Without Enemies*. Oxford: Polity Press, 1998.

Beck, Ulrich, Anthony Giddens, and Scott Lash. *Reflexive Modernization: Politics, Tradition and Aesthetics in the Modern Social Order*. Stanford, CA: Stanford University Press, 1994.

Brashares, Ann. "Under the Covers." In *New York Times*, Sunday, July 31, 2005.

Brueggemann, Walter. *Hopeful Imagination*. Philadelphia: Fortress Press, 1986.

Brueggemann, Walter. *Texts Under Negotiation*. Minneapolis: Augsburg Fortress Publishers, 1993.

Burke, Spencer. *Making Sense of Church*. Grand Rapids: Zondervan/EmergentYS, 2003.

Castells, Manuel. "The Information Age: Economy, Society and Culture." In *The Emergence of the Network Society*. 2nd ed., Vol. 1. Maldon, MA: Blackwell Publishers, 2000.

Ciulla, Joanne B. *The Working Life*. New York: Times/Random, 2000.

Conner, Daryl R. *Leading at the Edge of Chaos*. New York: John Wiley & Sons, Inc., 1998.

Geertz, Clifford. *The Interpretation of Cultures*. New York: Basic Books, 1973.

Guder, Darrel and Lois Barrett, eds. *Missional Church: A Vision for the Sending of the Church in North America*. Grand Rapids: William B. Eerdmans Publishing Company, 1998.

Handy, Charles. *The Hungry Spirit*. New York: Broadway, 1999.

Heifetz, Ronald A. and Marty Linsky. *Leadership on the Line: Staying Alive Through the Dangers of Leading*. Harvard: Harvard Business School Press, 2002.

Hiebert, Paul. *Anthropological Insights for Missionaries*. Grand Rapids: Baker, 1985.

Jacobs, Jane. *Dark Ages Ahead*. Toronto: Random House Canada, 2004.

Leddy, Mary Jo. *Reweaving the Religious Life*. Mystic, CT: Twenty-Third Publications, 1990.

McLaren, Brian. *A New Kind of Christian*. San Francisco: Jossey-Bass, 2001.

McLaren, Brian. *The Stories We Find Ourselves In*. San Francisco: Jossey-Bass, 2003.

Meisek, Anthony C. and M. L. del Mastro. *The Rule of Benedict*. NY: Doubleday/Image Books, 1975.

Miller, Lawrence M. *From Barbarians to Bureaucrats*. New York: Fawcett Books, 1990.

Milton, Coalter, John Mulder, and Louis Weeks. *The Organizational Revolution: Presbyterians and American Denominationalism*. Louisville, KY: Westminster/John Knox Press, 1992.

Myers, Joseph R. *The Search to Belong: Rethinking Intimacy, Community and Small Groups*. Grand Rapids: Zondervan/EmergentYS, 2003.

O'Donohue, John. *Eternal Echoes*. New York: HarperCollins, 1999.

Pascale, Richard, Mark Milleman, and Linda Gioja. *Surfing the Edge of Chaos*. New York: Three Rivers Press, 2000.

Peterson, Eugene. *The Contemplative Pastor*. Grand Rapids: William B. Eerdmans Publishing Company, 1989.

Reich, Robert. *The Future of Success*. New York: Vintage, 2002.

Reno, R.R. *In the Ruins of the Church: Sustaining Faith in an Age of Diminished Christianity*. Grand Rapids: Brazos Press, 2002.

Roxburgh, Alan. *The Missionary Congregation, Leadership, & Liminality*. Harrisburg, PA: Trinity Press International, 1997.

Schein, Edgar H. *Organizational Culture and Leadership*. San Francisco: Jossey-Bass, 2004.

Schleiermacher, Frederich. *On Religion: Speeches to its Cultured Despisers*. Louisville, KY: Westminster John Knox Press, 1994.

Scudieri, Robert J. *The Apostolic Church*. St. Louis, MO: Lutheran Society for Missiology, 1995.

Sennett, Richard. *The Corrosion of Character*. New York: W. W. Norton & Company, 1998.

Sweet, Leonard, ed. *The Church in Emerging Culture*. Grand Rapids: Zondervan/EmergentYS, 2003.

Tuchman, Barbara. *The Guns of August*. Toronto: Ballantine, 1994.

Turner, Victor. *The Ritual Process*. Chicago: Aldine Publishing Company, 1974.

Ward, Graham. *Cities of God*. New York: Routledge, 2000.

ALAN J. ROXBURGH

 serves as Vice President for Allelon Canada and as such serves as the Director of The Allelon Missional Leadership Network (AMLN), a network of relationships and resources that create a movement of missional formation among leaders, local churches and training schools throughout the USA, Europe and Australia. He has over twenty-seven years of experience in church leadership and on seminary faculty. He was responsbile for teaching in the areas of leadership development and domestic missiology. He lives in Vancouver, Canada with his wife, Jane, who is a high school principal.

Some of his current projects involve the formation of a missional order and the development of The Allelon Center for Missional Leadership—a multi-site center that provides resources and training to missional leaders and church communities from a wide array of organizations and denominations throughout North America and the world.

(http://www.allelon.org/center_for_learning/)

Alan has pastored three congregations involving the redevelopment of a downtown, urban church and the planting of other congregations. As well as serving as the director of an urban training center focused on preparing seminary graduates for cross-cultural ministry in Canada and overseas, he has served as a seminary professor and the director of a center for mission and evangelism.

Alan teaches as an adjunct professor in seminaries in the U.S., Australia, and Europe. He has written several books, including: *Reaching a New Generation* (InterVarsity Press, 1993) and (Regent College Press, 1998); *Leadership, Liminality and the Missionary Congregation* (Trinity Press, 1998); *Crossing the Bridge: Leadership in a Time of Change* (Percept, 2000); and *Missional Leadership: Equipping Your Church to Serve a Changing World* (JosseyBass, Winter 2006). He was also a member of the writing team which authored *Missional Church: A Vision for the Sending of the Church in North America* (Eerdmans, 1998).

Alan leads conferences and seminars with denominations, congregations, and seminaries across North America and Australia, as well as consulting with each of these groups in the areas of leadership for missional transformation and methods of system transformation. Alan has been a leader in the *Gospel and Our Culture Network* (GOCN) as well as managing a GOCN-Lilly research project into the innovation of missional systems. He is currently working in consulting relationships with several schools on issues of curriculum development and leadership design as well as consulting with a number of denominational organizations.

When not traveling or writing, Alan enjoys mountain biking, hiking, cooking, and hanging out with Jane and the grandchildren as well as drinking great coffee in the Pacific Northwest.

CONTACT INFORMATION:

E-mail: alan@allelon.org